FIRST EDITION APRIL 2019



PRINT EDITION

ISBN: 9781092506113

Written by Amanda Day Rose & Samantha Altieri
Illustrations by Amanda Day Rose

# BALANCED EATS

*A Book of Habits, Tips & Recipes for a Balanced Lifestyle*

RETHINK YOUR RELATIONSHIP WITH FOOD

# TABLE OF CONTENTS

## INTRODUCTION



## FINDING YOUR BALANCE



## CALORIES, MACRONUTRIENTS & MEAL TEMPLATE



## STRATEGIES TO SUCCEED



## MEAL PREPPING & PLANNING 101



## RECIPES

# WHY WE WROTE THIS FOR YOU

Hello food-loving friend, Amanda and Sam here! We are so glad you found us.. Now go grab yourselves a cup of coffee or tea (or wine!) and let's dive in.

Do you struggle with food? Maybe you've been yo-yo dieting since you can remember. Maybe meal-prepping or eating vegetables overwhelms you. Or maybe you eat clean on the weekdays but then by the time Friday rolls around, you lose all control and say "screw it" from restricting yourself and you binge eat.

Whatever you are struggling with, please just know that you are not alone and that is why we wrote this book!

We want you to think back to before you ever dieted. If you are anything like us, it's been a while, maybe since you were a young kid. You ate when you were hungry, you stopped when you were full and you ate everything you wanted in moderation. Ah, seems easy, right?

Unfortunately, food has not been easy for either of us. We've struggled with years of yo-yo dieting, losing and regaining the same 5,10, and even 20+ lbs, and not knowing how to change our bodies despite working out in the gym. But after years of struggling with food, we know that it is possible for you to enjoy your life, feel and look good, while enjoying your favorite foods because we have both gotten to a place where we practice it daily. We know that meal planning shouldn't consume your life and tracking calories isn't a requirement for feeling good or staying lean.

Our book, *Balanced Eats*, includes more than 15 years of combined experience in the kitchen and practicing (we are still working on it!) a balanced lifestyle.

If you are struggling, we get it. For a long time, our mindset around food was damaged. Sam struggled with emotional/stress eating and wavering between cycles of clean, restricted weekday eating followed by weekend binges. Amanda had a history of ignoring her cravings and hunger cues and struggling to give herself permission to enjoy more fun foods. Ultimately, our struggles were mostly in our head - we were telling ourselves a story that was sabotaging our fat loss efforts.

When we realized how many of you struggle with the same thing, we decided we wanted to write this book to help you re-learn how to eat, mend your relationship with food and eliminate the dieting mindset you've recited to yourself for the past years. You have the power to rewrite your story, and our book, *Balanced Eats*, will help you do just that.

Sam Altieri is a NASM-certified personal trainer, Precision Nutrition coach and owns Balance with Sam, where she coaches clients all over the world on mindset, nutrition, training and building a balanced lifestyle. She currently lives in Boston, MA but has a thing for the west coast (hey California, I'm coming for you!) Sam has a hard time deciding what she loves most: lifting weights, doing yoga or going for walks outside, but she knows she loves fish tacos, baby carrots, blueberry cake donuts and a nice glass of Malbec!

Amanda Rose is a personal trainer and teaches a class for women on how to properly lift weights. She is also a digital illustrator and recipe creator. She currently lives in Halifax, VA and has 4 cows, 4 dogs, 2 cats and ducks (aka an unlimited supply of duck eggs!). She has a major crush on pizza, grapefruit IPA, and Brussels sprouts.

Much love and cheers to balance!
xx, Amanda & Sam! <3

## INSTAGRAM

Sam Altieri: @saltylifts | Amanda Rose: @amandadayrose
www.balanced-eats.com

# PYRAMID OF HEALTH & WELLNESS

## MINDSET & SELF-CARE

*Mindset*

A strong body starts with a strong mind. Be more self-aware and intentional with your thoughts and your body will follow suit!

*Self Care*

Without health, you have nothing. Prioritize your overall well-being before anything else. You can't pour from an empty cup. Some stress relievers are taking a break from dieting, meditiating, getting quality sleep, spending time in nature, doing yoga or stretching, deep breathing, leisurely walking and social connection.

## NUTRITION & CALORIES

*Food Quality*

We recommend eating all foods you love in moderation. Aim to fill up on and eat healthy, more nutritious foods 80-85% of the time and then you can make room for fun, less nutritious foods 15-20% of the time.

*Calories*

Overall calorie intake will determine your body composition. Eat more calories than your body requires, you will gain weight. Eat less calories than your body needs, you will lost weight.
Protein: Protein is critical to maintain your muscle mass, to recover from workouts and to satiate you. If you are trying to lose weight, eating enough protein is necessary in order for the weight loss to be primarily fat, not muscle.

## SLEEP AND STRESS MANAGEMENT

*Sleep*

Aim for 7-9 hours per night. Getting enough sleep increases your quality of life, productivity, ability to lose fat, manage hunger, your energy and mood. A lack of sleep negatively impacts your brain, your hormones and your ability to recover.

*Stress & Recovery*

You need to balance your stressors with stress relievers. Even exercise is stress on the body, so taking your recovery seriously will help you prevent burnout and injury. Some stressors are dieting, long work hours, lack of sleep, negative self-talk, poor food choices, intense exercise and excessive caffeine or alcohol.

## MOVEMENT

*Lifting Weights*

Incorporating some sort of strength training 2-5x a week is a great way to build/maintain strength, prevent injuries, boost metabolism, change body composition, increase cognitive abilities and even slow the aging process.

*Cardio*

Our bodies are meant to move. Find active hobbies or start building a lifestyle that includes movement. Work your way up to 10,000 steps per day if you aren't participating in any cardio.

## WATER INTAKE

Aim for a minimum of ½ of your bodyweight in ounces. Ex: If you weigh 200lbs, aim for at least 100 ounces of water. If you are active or live in a warmer climate, we recommend aiming closer to 1 ounce per pound of bodyweight. Our general recommendation is to work your way up to one gallon per day!

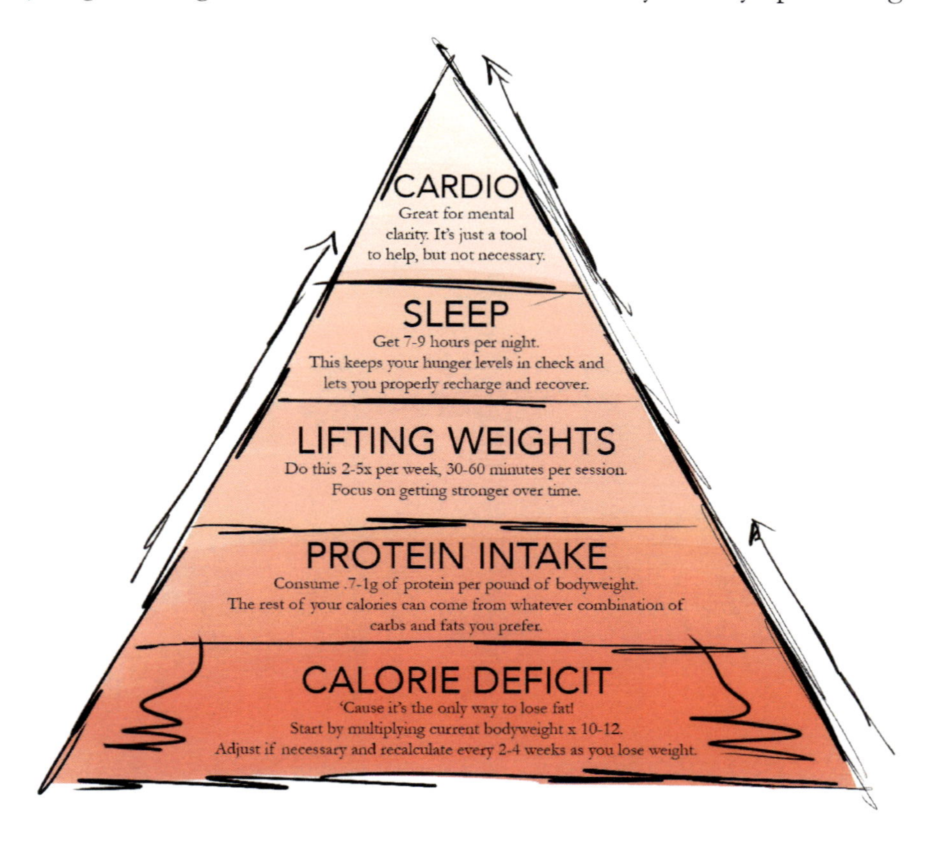

# FINDING YOUR BALANCE

*Life is like riding a bicycle. To keep your balance, you must keep moving.*

**ALBERT EINSTEIN**

# MINDSET & A BALANCED DIET

Have you ever been told that certain foods are good or bad, unhealthy or healthy? We used to believe that, but instead of seeing food in black and white terms, we encourage you to see food on a sliding scale from more nutritious (the foods you eat most) to more delicious (the foods you eat occasionally).

We want you to know that no food is inherently bad. Any food can be consumed in moderation as part of a healthy diet. Portions must be controlled when consuming more palatable and fun foods, because it is easier to overeat these foods, but they have a place in a balanced diet.

If your diet is primarily (80-85%) whole foods, you can include foods that you really love and might not be as nutritious, but provide you with happiness, mental sanity and allow you to more easily enjoy social settings.

Of course, we want you to feel good, but eating clean 100% is not realistic, not attainable and can come back to bite you in the butt!

**There will always be holidays, parties, work events or family gatherings. So we want you to get used to eating in a way that allows you to enjoy them. Remember, what you do most of the time matters much more than what you do once in a while.**

If you give yourself permission to enjoy the foods you want in moderation, you won't feel the need to eat like it's your last meal when the next event pops up on your calendar.

LET'S LOOK AT AN EXAMPLE:

You're given the option to choose a slice of cake worth 500 calories or 500 calories worth of protein, veggies and starchy carbs.

*If you had to pick, which would you choose?*

The cake gives you immediate gratification. It is good for the soul but will spike blood sugar, increase your chance of wanting more sweets and leave you hungry soon after.

A protein, veggie and carb combo has a higher nutritious value, a lower glycemic index and will fill you up for hours afterward.

Both, which may be the most sustainable approach. You enjoy a slightly smaller portion of the protein, veggie and carb combo, and enjoy a few bites of cake, leaving you with the best of both worlds.

So, the biggest tip we can share is to figure out what's worth it to you, be consistent, eat for health 80-85% of the time and then go enjoy your damn life the other 15-20%.

**BALANCE!**

# THE POWER OF REAL FOOD

We suggest opting for real food when possible. Eating real food will help you feel satisfied and provide you with more macronutrients (protein, fat and carbs), micronutrients, and food volume to fill you up. Whole foods will leave you feeling great after you eat them compared to calorically dense, processed or packaged foods!

It's taken us a while to find a balanced way to eat that is sustainable and we could picture doing for life! For years, we both ate 100% clean and would find ourselves in a vicious cycle that involved binge eating on the weekends due to restriction.

To save you from this, we want to emphasis the importance of including fun foods in your diet, not just on weekends, but throughout the week. By giving yourself permission to eat the things you love in moderation, the weekends won't sabotage your efforts.

There are sacrifices you will need to make, but with practice, you will find the fun foods and drinks that you love and want to keep in your diet.

FOR EXAMPLE:

Sam loves ice cream, whiskey and red wine. If she wants ice cream for dessert or knows she is going out and wants to have a glass of whiskey or enjoy a glass of Malbec, she will reduce her carbs at dinner to accommodate that! Or, she will make a healthier alternative to the ice cream, like blending frozen bananas!

Amanda loves pizza and IPAs. If she's craving pizza, she will make it at home and save herself a greasy pizza hangover. Or, rather than having her typical portion of starchy carbs at dinner, she will fill her plate with veggies and protein and enjoy the IPA (or maybe a few lighter beers), guilt-free.

At the end of the day, it's about making sacrifices and figuring out what's worth keeping in your diet for you and your preferences. Experiment with different foods to find the ones that satisfy you and keep you feeling good.

# CULTIVATING YOUR MINDSET AROUND FOOD

For a long time, the story we told ourselves was ultimately sabotaging our fat loss efforts because our mindset around food was damaged.

After working with our own coaches, we started reciting some mantras to rewire our thoughts and to reduce, and eventually eliminate, our need to use food to cope with stress or emotions.

Here are some of our food mindset mantras that we encourage you to recite to yourself. You can write them down and put them in a highly visible place so you constantly remember to say them to yourself.

*I know that food is not the answer to my problems.*
*I eat when I'm hungry, not due to stress or emotion.*
*I can always have more later.*
*I give myself permission to enjoy things I love.*
*I am allowed to say no to foods that are offered to me.*
*I can eat anything I want, in moderation.*
*I know that hunger is not an emergency.*
*I eat 3-4 big, filling, satisfying meals a day and don't snack.*
*I drink a glass of water before and after each meal.*
*I experience hunger for 30-60 minutes before eating.*

Repeating these mantras can help you create a healthier approach to food and overcome your own self-sabotage.

# SAM & AMANDA'S HEALTHY HABITS

### 3-4 MEALS PER DAY WITH NO SNACKS

I prefer to eat 3 bigger meals that satisfy me and don't leave me hungry an hour later. I give myself permission to add my favorite sauces or toppings and then feel totally satiated.

---

### THE ONE BIG PLATE RULE

I use a 9" plate or 6" bowl and load my plate up! I prioritize lean protein and veggies. I view my plate as a pie chart diagram: ½ veggies, ¼ protein, ¼ starchy carbs and fats. Even when I go out to eat, I make sure that at least half of my plate is veggies so that I feel full without feeling heavy.

---

### ELIMINATE OR REDUCE LIQUID CALORIES

With the exception of unsweetened almond or cashew milk, a glass of whiskey or red wine, I don't drink my calories. I prefer to eat food. I drink 3-4 liters of water per day, lots of coffee (black or with nut-based milk and a dash of stevia) and lots of sparkling water!

---

### EXPERIENCE TRUE HUNGER BEFORE MEALS

To avoid eating emotionally, my goal is to experience a hollow feeling in my stomach for about 30-60 minutes before eating. I'm not always perfect with this, but I try to be as aware of my hunger cues as possible to avoid eating for anything other than hunger.

---

### NEVER HAVE A "BAD" MEAL TWICE

If we slip up, we get back on track for our next meal. We try not to beat ourselves up about it and remind ourselves that consistency is much more important than perfection. We ditched the all-or-nothing mentality and instead of saying, "screw it - we already messed up, mind as well keep screwing up," we now view each meal as an opportunity to practice good habits and just get back on track.

---

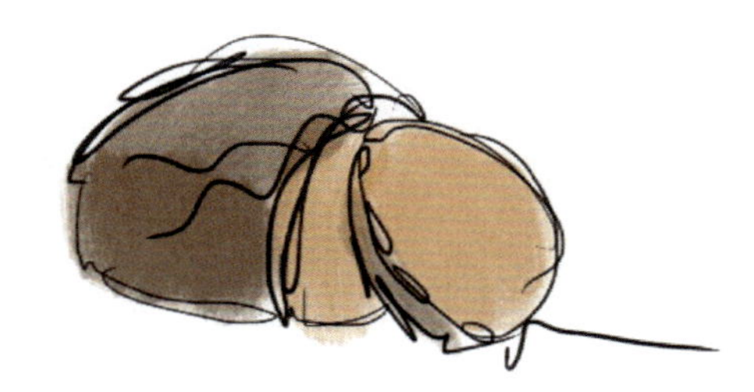

### SNEAK VEGETABLES IN WHEREVER POSSIBLE

Vegetables are PACKED with micronutrients – the nutrients we tend to forget about because we're so focused on our macros and calorie count as a whole. But those micronutrients are essential for our health, and generally just make us feel good, so it's important to make sure we're getting enough of them. An easy way to get lots of micronutrient-packed vegetables is to sneak them into your daily meals. Add spinach to your protein shakes (you won't even taste it, I promise!) or diced carrots to marinara sauce.

---

## PORTION OUT SERVINGS RATHER THAN EATING FROM CONTAINERS

I have a history of binge eating and this helps me stay on track and be realistic and mindful of portions. I know myself well enough to know that I can't just eat from a bag of chips or a pint of ice cream and not finish it. To prevent self-sabotage, I do what I need to do to stay on track and feel in control!

---

## USE COOKING SPRAY OR OLIVE OIL IN A SPRAY BOTTLE

Extra virgin olive oil and avocado oil are great for cooking but can add hundreds of calories when poured directly in the pan. Be mindful of the heaviness of your pour or opt to cook foods using methods like steaming, baking, roasting or via slow cooker or pressure cooker.

---

## KEEP A NOTEBOOK OF YOUR MEAL PLANS

Amanda keeps her grocery lists and weekly meal plans in a notebook that is kept in a kitchen drawer and Sam prefers to free-style it or use the Notes app in her phone. Either way, making a game plan is great especially when life gets crazy and meal prep is the first thing to go out the window. You can go back to a previous week's list and just use that one all over again (or combine meals from several plans to make a fresh, new plan!).

---

## HAVE A FEW GO-TO MEALS THAT YOU LOVE

It will be much easier to stay on track and work towards your goals when you have several healthy meals up your sleeve that you absolutely love. We love protein oatmeal for breakfast so much, and if you have a few meals you love in your back pocket, you'll instantly gravitate towards those when you're craving something!

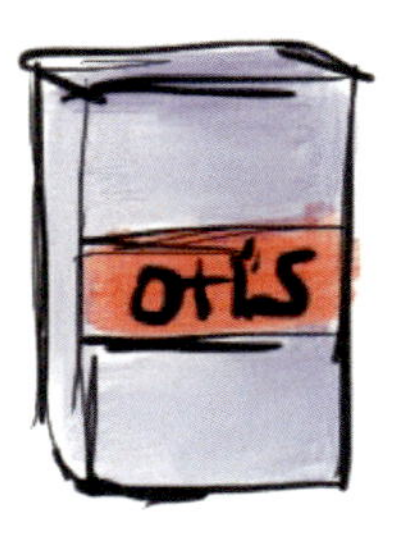


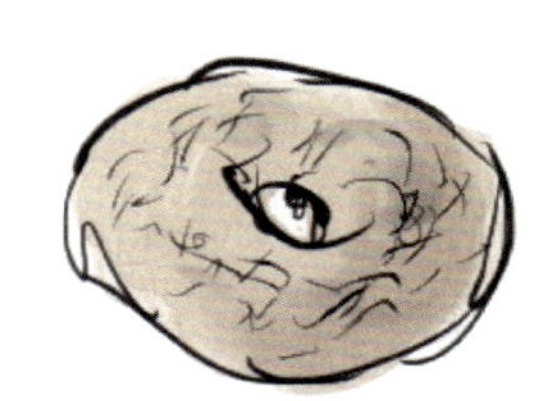

# CALORIES, MACRONUTRIENTS & MEAL TEMPLATE

*Do not skip meals. Eat three meals a day and eat until you feel satisfied and comfortably full.*

**SUZANNE SOMERS**

# CALCULATING YOUR CALORIES BASED ON YOUR GOAL

If you've never counted calories before, we suggest that you try it for a few weeks! You don't need to do it forever, but counting calories is a great skill to have so that you are aware of what is actually in the foods you are eating and how they make you feel. If you don't know how much you currently eat, how will you know what direction you are heading?

If you don't want to track calories, as previously mentioned, you can use your hand to determine portion sizes for you. If you do feel comfortable and want to keep track of calories, here's the formula you can use:

### FAT LOSS

*Multiply bodyweight (in lbs) x 10-12*

Aim for the lower end of the range (10) if you aren't active or have a sedentary lifestyle and aim for the higher end of the range (12) if you have an active lifestyle and training schedule.

---

### MAINTENANCE

*Multiply bodyweight (in lbs) x 14*

This will differ person to person, but (14) is a good starting point. If you aren't currently tracking calories and have maintained your bodyweight and physique for a while, another option is to record what you are currently eating for a few weeks. The average calories will most likely be your maintenance calories.

---

### GAINING MUSCLE

*Multiply bodyweight (in lbs) x 16-18*

Aim for the lower end of the range (16) if you aren't active or have a sedentary lifestyle and aim for the higher end of the range (18) if you have an active lifestyle, training schedule, have a hard time gaining weight or you have a fast metabolism.

There is no "perfect" calorie number. We encourage you to pick a number and eat within that range consistently for a few weeks and adjust from there depending on the results!

Ex: You weigh 200lbs. You are trying to lose fat, so you should aim for 2000-2400 calories per day. Eat within that range for a few weeks and see what happens. 400 calories can seem like a big range, so be sure to adjust depending on your activity level. You don't need to be perfect with this, but you need to be consistent.

## *Consistency > Perfection*

It's better to eat within a larger calorie range 100% of the time rather than aiming for perfection and hitting your exact calorie number once in a while. It's simple, yes. But it's not always easy.

Keep in mind, all of these calculations will be rough estimates and you will probably need to adjust. There is not one-size-fits-all, so give yourself plenty of time to test each range. Don't increase/decrease calories every few days because you get frustrated. Let the process happen! Each person has specific calories needs depending on their bodyweight, muscle mass, training volume, dieting history, metabolism and genetics.

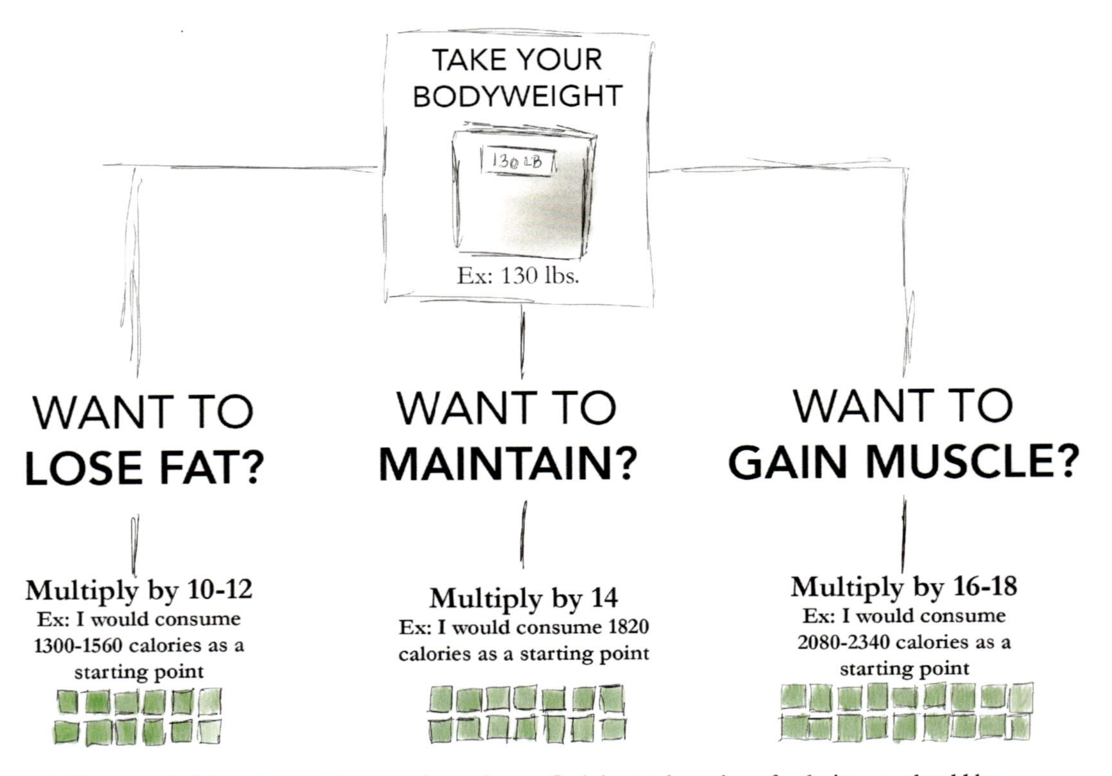


****Keep in mind that these are just starting points to find the total number of calories you should be eating per day to support your goals. Realistically, you need to track your calorie intake and monitor changes in bodyweight to determine if you need to be eating more or less calories to reach your goals at a healthy rate. Healthy fat loss happens at at a rate of .5-1lb per week, on average.**

# MACRONUTRIENTS & CALCULATING YOUR OWN

There are three major macronutrients that the human body needs in order to function properly:
PROTEIN, FATS, AND CARBOHYDRATES

*1 gram of protein = 4 calories*
*1 gram of carbohydrate = 4 calories*
*1 gram of fat = 9 calories*

## PROTEIN (4 CALORIES PER GRAM)

*How much? (.7-1g of protein per pound of bodyweight; ex: 100lb person needs 70-100grams)*

Protein is made up of amino acids, which are the building blocks of life and critical to keep our body functioning properly. It helps us maintain optimal body composition, maintain strong immunity, performance, healthy metabolism, and helps to repair and replace cells that have been worn out.

Consuming a higher level of protein is critical for adequate recovery for workouts and will help you feel satisfied after eating.

## CARBOHYDRATES (4 CALORIES PER GRAM)

*How much? See calculator below.*

Carbs, both simple and complex, are the main sources of energy for all of your body's cells. We recommend getting a majority of your carbohydrates from complex carbs like vegetables and fruits.

As your activity level and muscle mass increases, your requirements for carbohydrates will also increase.

Simple carbs are higher glycemic and are broken down more rapidly by the body, causing a spike of insulin. These simple sugars and refined carbs are things like cereal, candy, white flour and white pasta.

Complex carbs are lower glycemic, broken down by the body more slowly, increase vitamin and mineral intake, contribute to fiber intake, enhances satiety, and better controls blood sugar. 25 grams of fiber/day is a great real of thumb. Complex carbs are things like vegetables, legumes, fruits, nuts, seeds, and whole grains.

### FAT (9 CALORIES PER GRAM)

*How much? See calculator below.*

Dietary fat is the most calorically dense macronutrient, at 9 calories per gram. Compared to carbs and protein, your body has the easiest time digesting and storing fat as body fat. Dietary fat is more calorie-dense and less satiating than protein or carbs.

Sometimes fat gets a bad rap, but consuming enough fat will help to keep you feeling full between meals and it gives us energy and helps to absorb vitamins such as vitamins A, D, E, and K. We need healthy fats to keep our metabolism in check, promote health immune system, and hormone production.

Focus on getting quality healthy fats in your diet for best results. Refer to our macro cheat sheet.

---

### SAMPLE CALORIE AND MACRONUTRIENT CALCULATOR

*Sam is 5'2" and weighs 130lbs. In this scenario, let's say she has a highly active lifestyle and is looking to lose fat.*

**Calories: 130 x 10-12 = 1300-1560 calories/day**

---

*Remember how we mentioned that the calorie calculations listed were just a starting range? Because Sam is highly active, walks 10-15,000 steps per day and has higher amounts of muscle mass than a beginner, her calorie deficit may be less severe due to a more active lifestyle (more calories burned/day).*

*Let's use 1500-1600 calories as her calorie deficit for this example.*

PROTEIN

**130 x .7-1g = 91 - 130 grams/day [520 calories]**

*Sam prefers to eat 125-130 grams per day, as she knows protein helps to satiate her and keep her full between meals. Eating at the higher end of this range also helps to maintain as much muscle mass as possible when losing weight.*

CARBS & FATS

This is totally up to you! With whatever calories you have left, we suggest 20%-30% of your calories from fats and 40-55% of your calories from carbs, depending on your preferences.

**1600 calories [total calories]**
**- 520 calories [protein]**
**1080 calories left to split between carbs and fats**

*Sam prefers a balanced ratio of fats and carbs, but it fluctuates day to day. Sometimes, she will eat more avocado or peanut butter, some days, she will crave more carbs. At the end of the day, it's about being flexible and focusing your efforts on consistently reaching your overall calories and protein target.*

**PRO TIP**

Focus on getting enough protein at each meal to keep you full throughout the day. Your carbs and fats can then fall anywhere within your caloric goals.

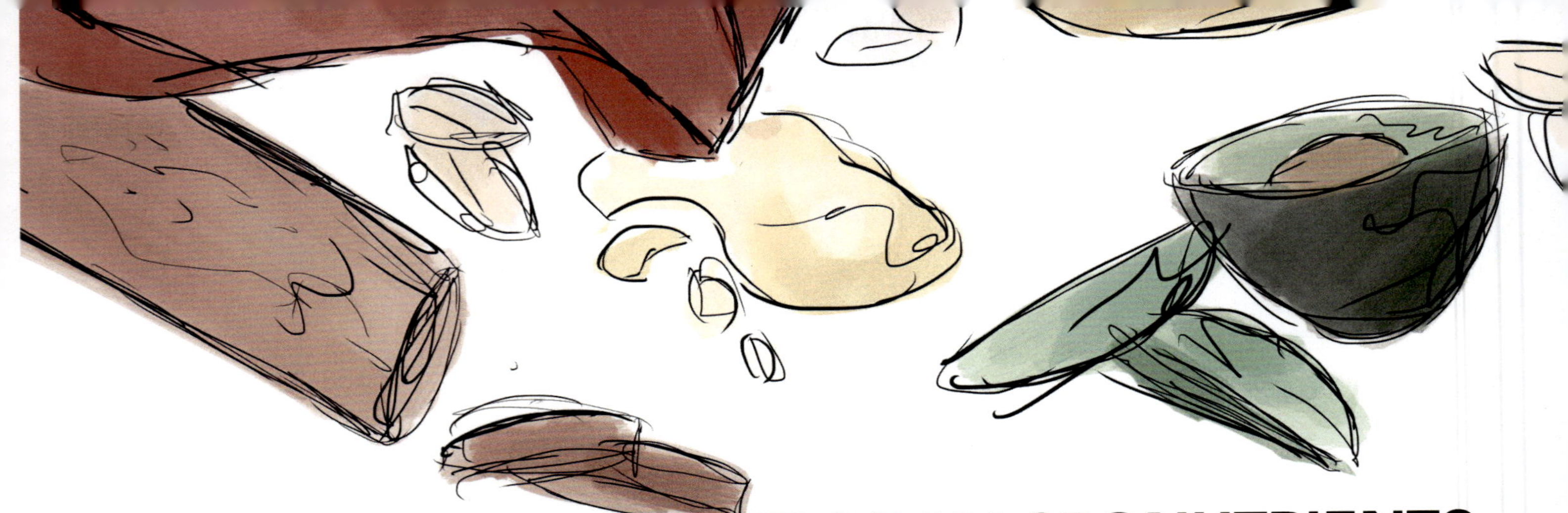

# THE MEGA LIST OF MACRONUTRIENTS

| PROTEIN | CARBOHYDRATES | FAT |
| --- | --- | --- |
| Chicken breast | Bread | Avocados |
| Turkey breast | Beans | Butter |
| Pork | Oats | Nuts |
| Ground beef | Quinoa | Eggs |
| Ground turkey | Barley | Olives |
| Ground Chicken | Broccoli | Coconut |
| Sausage | Legumes | Salmon |
| Bacon | Chickpeas | Sardines |
| Venison | White potatoes | Mackerel |
| Shrimp | Sweet potatoes | Nut butters |
| Cod | Carrots | Olive oil |
| Salmon | Yogurt | Coconut oil |
| Cheese | Pineapple | Avocado oil |
| Collagen | Bananas | Fish oil |
| Cottage cheese | Apples | Cheese |
| Protein powder | Pears | Full-fat yogurt |
| Greek yogurt | Pasta | Chia seeds |
| Black beans | Corn | Pumpkin seeds |
| Kidney beans | Popcorn | Ground flaxseed |
| Lima beans | Milk | Dark chocolate |
| Chickpeas | Rice | |
| Green peas | Pasta | |
| Leafy greens | Teff | |
| Edamame | Cereal | |
| Lentils | Bagels | |
| Quinoa | Candy | |
| Tempeh | Baked goods | |
| Tofu | Beer | |
| Hemp seeds | Wine | |
| Chia seeds | | |

# MEAL TEMPLATE, CREATING YOUR PLATE & PROPER PORTIONS

Does counting calories cause you stress or anxiety? Maybe it leaves you feeling overwhelmed because you want to hit your numbers perfectly?

We both used to get anxious about tracking food and it started to consume us. If that sounds like you, we recommend stepping away from tracking calories for a while and learning how to eat using habits.

We recommend eating 3-4 bigger meals and using your hand and our handy plate diagram! Using these tools can help you keep your portions in check and in alignment with your goals.

Not sure when or how often to eat? We suggest eat whenever you prefer and are most hungry. If you tend to get hungrier later at night, shift your meals to later in the day. Breakfast is not a requirement. If you are hungry upon awakening, eat breakfast. If you don't have an appetite upon awakening, hold off on eating until you get hungry. Figure out when YOU tend to be hungriest (morning or night) and let your diet work with you.

HOW TO CREATE YOUR PLATE FOR EACH MEAL

**Protein: Women: 1 palm / Men: 2 palms**
**Carbs (Fibrous): Women: 1 fist / Men: 2 fists**
**Carbs (Starchy): Women: 1 cupped hand / Men: 2 cupped hands**
**Fat: Women: 1 thumb at most meals / Men: 2 thumbs**

Keep in mind that using your hand for portions is a starting point! You may have to increase or decrease portions based on hunger, activity level, height, weight and your goals. The key is to be aware of how you feel after each meal and adjust accordingly. Refer back to our hunger scale and aim to feel a 4-6 for satiety.

Neither of us currently track calories because we don't want the added stress. Like we've mentioned previously, if you've never counted calories, we do recommend it for at least a month because it is a skill that you will have for life that will bring awareness to you and your habits.

While you don't need to count calories to see progress, counting calories may provide you with more accurate results. Whatever you decide to do, just know you don't need to do it forever. You are in control and can always go through phases of tracking and phases of habit-based eating.

# MEAL TEMPLATE FOR FAT LOSS

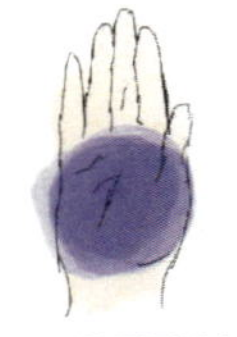

PROTEIN

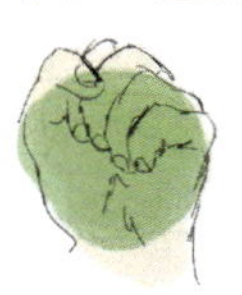

VEGGIES

STARCHY CARBS

FAT

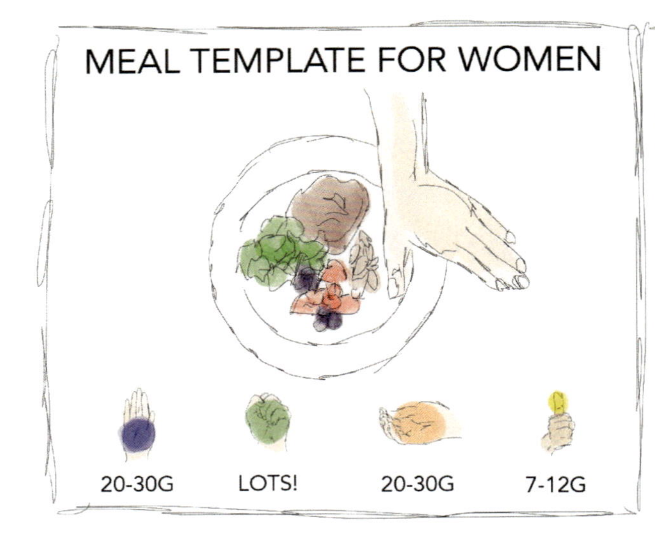


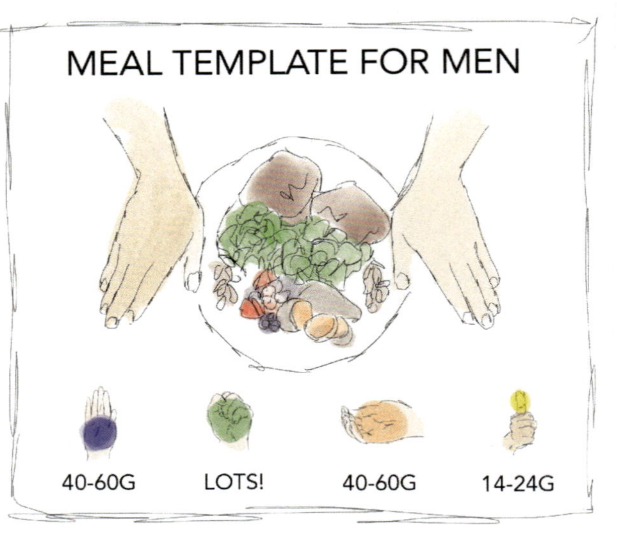


Your hand is related to your body size. It's portable and a personalized way to measure and track food intake. Keep in mind that this is a starting point! Stay flexible and adjust portions based on hunger, fullness, training volume, and goals.

# TRACKING CALORIES & MEASURING FOOD

## WHY TRACK YOUR FOOD INTAKE?

Tracking your food allows you to see the trends in your diet and see the big picture. You may think you are eating enough protein (we sure did!) or eating enough vegetables, but how will you know the truth unless you track it?

The harsh reality is that most people are not reaching their protein requirements and consuming too many carbs and fats, typically due to packaged foods. Portion sizes have increased over time and some restaurants serve portions that are 2-3 times the amount that an average person needs in one sitting. Lots of times, these meals are focused on carbs and fats with less (or no!) emphasis on protein or vegetables.

We recommend logging your food for at least a month so you can get a more honest and accurate representation of your total daily intake of calories and macronutrients. When you have awareness, then you can take action and modify your eating to support your goals.

We recommend an app like MyFitnessPal or using a journal to log food. Though MyFitnessPal is very easy to use and has an incredibly large food database with lots of restaurant menus, it's not for everyone. You can also look up nutritional data for most foods on a website like www.calorieking.com.

Keeping track of portions can be done using your hand, measuring cups, or a scale, in order from least accurate to most accurate.

### USING YOUR HAND

Eyeballing portions is easy, free, and portable, but is the least accurate.

---

### MEASURING CUPS

Volume measurements are easy, but may become time-consuming.

---

### FOOD SCALE

Weight measurements are the most accurate but may be impractical, especially when you are away from home.

---

When you are home, we recommend using a food scale to see how inaccurate the other methods can be, and as you get more familiar and experienced, you can switch to easier, less accurate methods.

If you are measuring your portions wrong everyday, those calories can add up quick and may prevent you from losing fat! It's the compound effect that truly matters, not the one-off instance of measuring incorrectly.

**We recommend measuring things like nuts, nut butters, pasta, grains, and any other fats.** When eyeballing these foods, it's easy to go overboard or overestimate portions. Because fats are more calorically dense, they make the biggest impact if compounded day-to-day. When we first measured our peanut butter by weight, we realized that when we used measuring spoons, we were unintentionally consuming 1.5 or even 2 tablespoons, not the 1 tablespoon that we originally thought. So, do us a favor and learn from our mistakes to save yourself a lot of frustration!

# CONVERSION CHART

| CUPS | TABLESPOONS | GRAMS | OUNCES |
|---|---|---|---|
| 1/4 C. | 4 TBSP. | 57 G | 2 OZ. |
| 1/2 C. | 8 TBSP. | 114 G | 4 OZ. |
| 2/3 C. | 11 TBSP. | 141 G | 5 OZ. |
| 3/4 C. | 12 TBSP. | 170 G | 6 OZ. |
| 1 C. | 16 TBSP. | 228 G | 8 OZ. |
| 2 C. | 32 TBSP. | 456 G | 16 OZ. |
| 4 C. | 64 TBSP. | 912 G | 32 OZ. |

# STRATEGIES TO SUCCEED

*People who succeed have momentum. The more they succeed,*
*the more they want to succeed, and the more they find a way to succeed.*

**TONY ROBBINS**

# WHAT WE EAT IN A DAY

Eating should be enjoyable! Food is meant to taste good and we want you to look forward to meals that satisfy you. If you don't already, we suggest having a few staple meals in your back pocket.

We recommend having 2-3 breakfasts and 4-5 dinners in your "meal library" that you really enjoy and align with your goals, as it will help you stay on track and simplify eating.

We eat a lot of the same foods day-to-day because we enjoy them, it's less decisions we have to make throughout the day, we know exactly what we need to buy at the grocery store, and we know how to prepare them and how long it takes to prep them.

If you don't have staple meals yet, take a look at what you've eaten in the past few weeks. Do you see trends? Are you a creature of habit or do you like trying new things? Find what works for you!

Jot down your favorite foods (hint: use the pages at the end of this book!) and figure out how to make healthier versions of the things you love!

STEPS TO SUCCESS

**Pick a meal frequency that works for you (we prefer 3 bigger meals)**
**Get a meal library together (6-8 meals you love)**
**Compile recipes and adjust recipes if needed to align with your goals**
**Go to the grocery store & prep food!**
**Repeat the cycle each week**

The graphic below shows a typical day of eating for both of us! We both eat the things we do because we genuinely enjoy them, look forward to eating them, they are tasty as hell and they support our goals. Simple as that!

---

SAM'S FAVORITE DAY OF EATING

PB&J Oatmeal + Lots o' Coffee
Cheesy Pasta Skillet with Spicy Sausage
1 Egg + Egg White Omelet and Avocado Toast

AMANDA'S FAVORITE DAY OF EATING

Snickerdoodle Oatmeal + Lots o' Coffee
Brussel Sprouts Salad with Turkey Sausage
Peanut Chicken Stir Fry

# MANAGING HUNGER

Most of us only know two extremes of eating: starving or stuffed. Very rarely do we actually slow down to mindfully eat our food, be aware of our hunger levels, our body and its cues.

The hunger scale can help you to visually think about your physical sensation as it pertains to hunger. Being more aware of hunger can help you manage portion sizes, eat only when hungry, not as a response to emotions or stress, understand when to stop eating and recognize your unique hunger cues.

*Try practicing eliminating hunger, NOT chasing fullness.*

ZONES 1-3

Try to stay out of these zones to avoid binging, overeating, or becoming ravenous or lightheaded.

ZONES 4-7

The sweet spot of fullness. Zone 5-6 is where you want to be after a meal. Like you could eat more but feel good.

ZONES 8-10

Try to avoid this zone! This is what you may typically feel like after big meals like Thanksgiving

Something that we have had to relearn is that hunger is not an emergency. If you don't like the food options presented to you, you don't have to eat them. You are responsible and in control of what you eat and drink. No one is forcing you to eat things you don't want to (unless you have a crazy friend who thinks it's fun to force feed you!) Just remember, you can always eat later and you are in control.

Hunger is a normal sensation and doesn't need to be satisfied right way. Just like being tired, it doesn't mean you need to immediately go to bed! If you are in an environment where the food options don't align with your goals, drink some water and distract yourself until you are surrounded by food that you know will make you feel good.

# OUR #1 TIP: VOLUME EATING

We believe that volume eating is the #1 strategy for staying on track, adhering to your goals and managing hunger. It keeps your calorie intake low while maximizing the amount of food that you can consume. Having permission to eat more food is always a win in our book!

Volume eating is a mental game-changer for us but also has lots of health benefits, too! The foods classified as most voluminous (see list below) are typically full of water, very nutrient dense, packed with fiber, vitamins, and minerals so you will stay hydrated and fueled.

We love big meals. There's something incredibly satisfying about giving yourself permission to eat and finish an entire plate of food and feel satisfied!

When we make our meals, we prioritize foods that are low glycemic and full of fiber. Some of our favorites are low-calorie veggies, oats, potatoes, whole eggs, fish, soup, steak, and fruit like berries and apples.

## HERE ARE SOME STRATEGIES FOR YOU

Veggify your meals! Load up on veggies in most meals. You don't need to give yourself a boring portion of broccoli, you can get creative and sneak them into meals, too! Add veggies to your sauces, omelets, stir fry, pasta dishes, casseroles, and even smoothies.

## HEALTHY SWAPS

Swap out starchy carbs for low calorie substitutes or do ½ portion of each. Instead of eating just 1 cup of white rice, use ½ cup white rice and ½ cup (or more) of cauliflower rice. Instead of pasta and sauce, try spaghetti squash or zucchini noodles.

## MAKE A SALAD!

Use our salad bowl template to learn how to eat a huge bowl of food, stay full for hours and load up on nutrients, vitamins and health.

## EAT LESS PROTEIN BARS, PROTEIN SHAKES AND REDUCE/ELIMINATE LIQUID CALORIES

Eating your food rather than drinking it will not only slow down your eating but will fill your stomach much more. Chewing your food rather than drinking it is a lot more mentally and physically satisfying.

## LOAD UP YOUR OATMEAL

One of our go-to hacks is to add cooked riced cauliflower to your oatmeal, which has no change in taste but adds volume and veggies or you can add egg whites, which gives your oatmeal a fluffy, cakey texture. You can even add grated pumpkin, carrots or zucchini. Make soups or stews which are incredibly low-calorie but packed with tons of health. This high-volume liquid-based food is hot in temperature which will cause you to slow down when eating, allow you to listen to your body and pay better attention to your hunger cues.

Be aware of the caloric density of your food and how satiated you will feel after eating it. High fat and low nutrition foods are usually where you run into issues of overeating.

## HIGH CALORIE FOODS

Most of these higher calorie foods are fats or a combo of carb/fats. Fats are calorically more dense (at 9 calories per gram, compared to protein/carb at 4 calories per gram) and are easier to overeat. It's okay to include these in your diet, just be mindful and accurate of your portions.

*Oils* — *Cheese*
*Butter* — *High-fat meats*
*Nuts* — *High-fat fish*
*Nut butter* — *Processed junk foods*
*Cream*

**PRO TIP**

Sub out half of your starchy carbs for vegetables. Use ½ rice and ½ veggie rice or ½ pasta and ½ veggies. This will provide you with more food volume but ½ the calories!

## LOW CALORIE (VOLUMINOUS) FOODS

*All calories listed per 100g unless otherwise stated

Vegetables:

*Broccoli (34 cal)*
*Cauliflower (25 cal)*
*Brussel Sprouts (43 cal)*
*Asparagus (20 cal)*
*Leafy Greens like Spinach, Kale, Bok Choy, Arugula and Lettuces (generally from 15-50 cal)*
*Artichokes (47 cal)*
*Mushrooms (22 cal)*

*Whole Green Beans (31 cal)*
*Turnips (28 cal)*
*Cabbage (25 cal)*
*Bell Peppers (20 cal)*
*Carrots (41 cal)*
*Zucchini (17 cal)*
*Hard Squashes like Acorn (40 cal), Butternut (45 cal), or Spaghetti (31 cal)*
*Cucumber (16 cal)*
*Tomato (18 cal)*
*Pickles (11 cal)*
*Sauerkraut (19 cal)*

Fruits:

*Strawberries (33 cal)*
*Watermelon (30 cal)*
*Melon (34 cal)*
*Grapefruit (42 cal)*
*Oranges (47 cal)*
*Peach (39 cal)*
*Blueberries (57 cal)*
*Raspberries (53 cal)*
*Blackberries (43 cal)*

Carbs:

*Cooked Oatmeal (68 cal)*
*Boiled Potato (77 cal)*
*Lentils (116 cal)*
*Edamame (122 cal)*
*Green Peas (81 cal)*
*Air Popped Popcorn (1 cup = 31 cal)*
*High Fiber Tortillas (1 tortilla = 90 cal)*
*Shirataki noodles (3 oz dry = 2 cal)*

Protein:

*Egg whites (52 cal)*
*Nonfat Greek yogurt (59 cal)*
*Nonfat cottage cheese (72 cal)*
*99% lean ground turkey (115 cal)*
*Boneless, skinless chicken breast (165 cal)*

# GETTING MORE PROTEIN & USING PROTEIN POWDER

Do you struggle getting enough protein? If you are an active individual, we recommend aiming for .7- 1g of protein per pound of bodyweight. (Ex: If you're 200lbs, 140-200g of protein.)

Lots of times it can be hard to hit your protein goal, and if that's the case for you, our biggest recommendation is to increase portion size of protein at meals.

Example: if you are currently eating 3oz. of cooked chicken (which has 125 calories and 25g of protein), opt for 4-5 oz! It will make eating more protein less of a chore, and it will just take up a bigger portion of your plate.

Another strategy is to use protein powder as a supplement to help you reach your protein goal. We don't recommend relying on it as your main protein source, but it's a great tool to help you reach your protein target. We suggest getting most of your protein from real food (eggs, lean meats, fish, beans, tofu, tempeh, etc) and then use a protein supplement to fill the gaps!

*Here are some ways to incorporate protein powder into your diet:*

PROTEIN SMOOTHIE

Add 1 scoop and blend

OATMEAL

Add 1 scoop and stir

YOGURT

Add 1/2-1 scoop and mix

PEANUT BUTTER

Mix 2-4 tbsp of any powdered peanut butter with 1/2 scoop of protein powder. Mix with water or plant based milk for an awesome spread. We eat this with apples or sometimes spread it on toast!

PROTEIN PANCAKES

Use protein powder instead of flour!

PROTEIN MUG CAKE

Use protein powder instead of flour!

Protein powder is a great substitute for flour in lots of baking recipes! Usually you can sub up to 1/3 of the flour in recipes for protein powder. It is a 1:1 ratio, but be sure to check the instructions for your recipe before you start scooping so you don't end up with a chalky desert.

**We love Bowmar Nutrition protein powder!**

# HOW TO EAT OUT & STAY ON TRACK

Eating out used to cause us stress or anxiety, especially if we were trying to stay on track. When we go out to eat, we have a few go-to strategies to help us feel good and enjoy ourselves!

Keep in mind, one meal out won't ruin your progress or cause you to gain fat, but if you are consistently eating out, it may be harder to keep portions in check and stay on track. Just like one salad won't make you healthy, one meal out won't make you fat.

When we go out, we approach it like any other meal. It's not an excuse to say "screw it," and sabotage all of the hard work you've been putting in earlier in the week.

**PRO TIP**

Don't show up to your meal starving. If you show up to a meal out ravenous, you will be much more likely to overeat and blow it! Sometimes we will have a small protein or veggie-centered snack beforehand to feel in control when showing up to dinner.

The best advice we can give is to PLAN! Regularly consuming foods outside of your "typical diet" in moderation will keep you mentally sane (always a good thing!) and will keep you social! It may also reduce the urge to binge eat or use the weekends as a time to self-sabotage.

### FOCUS ON THE EXPERIENCE OF A MEAL OUT AND WHO YOU ARE WITH!

Engage in conversation and enjoy your company.

### CHECK OUT THE MENU BEFOREHAND AND MAKE A PLAN.

Drink 1-2 glasses of water before your meal so you don't mistake thirst for hunger.

### EAT SLOWLY AND MINDFULLY, ONE BITE AT A TIME.

### MAKE YOUR MEALS PROTEIN-CENTERED.

### EAT LOTS OF GRILLED OR FRESH VEGGIES.

You can order a side salad, double up on veggies and or even ask your server to reduce/eliminate your portion of starchy carbs so you can enjoy dessert or a drink.

### PICK ONLY WHAT'S WORTH IT.

Are the appetizers calling your name? Or maybe the restaurant has your favorite dessert? Or you just want a glass of wine or a beer? Whatever it is, find what's most enjoyable for you. Give yourself permission to eat the things you really want and you'll be less likely to feel the need to eat it all.

*Remember, you are in control of what you eat. You will have to deal with what you eat/drink, not anyone else. Don't let anyone pressure you into eating something you don't want to.*

# MEAL PREPPING & PLANNING 101

*Context and memory play powerful roles in all the truly great meals in one's life.*

**ANTHONY BOURDAIN**

# GROCERY SHOPPING & MEAL PREP

If you don't go to the grocery store without a plan, you'll end up getting home, $200 later with ton of stuff you don't need/want in your house!

After many years of cooking and prepping, we wanted to share our habits and tips for staying on track:

### PLAN YOUR MEALS AND PICK YOUR DAY(S) TO MEAL PREP

We prefer Sunday afternoons and if we need an additional day, we opt for mid-week, like Wednesday nights.

### THINK OF MEAL PREP LIKE AN APPOINTMENT

It's a non-negotiable for your health, goals and wallet! Choose a few healthy meals to make for the week.

**PRO TIP**

Most of what you need will be on the outside perimeter of the grocery store. The middle aisles are usually packed with things you don't need!

### GO TO THE GROCERY STORE WITH A PLAN AND A LIST

This will help so you aren't tempted to bring foods into your home that will cause you to go off track. Don't buy or bring anything you don't want to be tempted to eat into the house. We love frozen veggies and fruit. They don't go bad, are typically cheaper than it's fresher alternative, and are just as tasty and packed with benefits.

### LET YOUR APPLIANCES DO THE WORK

Cook a few cups of quinoa or rice in a rice cooker and cook your protein in a crockpot. Take advantage of cooking methods that allow foods to excrete natural juices to increase the flavors of your meal without the extra calories.

### STORE FOOD IN CLEAR CONTAINERS SO YOU CAN SEE WHAT YOU HAVE IN THE FRIDGE

If you can see healthier foods, chances are, you'll actually eat them.

*We suggest using your meal library to help you stay consistent and know what you like and what makes your body feel good. Think of your grocery shopping in 5 parts:*

### PROTEIN

Opt for lean cuts and servings. Some of our favorites are egg whites, low fat chicken sausages, lean pork chops, and lean ground turkey (93-99%).

### CARBS (FIBROUS VEGGIES)

Load up on these low-calorie goodies for health and more food volume. We usually opt for lots of frozen veggies, leafy greens and dipping veggies like carrots, cucumbers, celery (but you definitely won't ever see celery in Amanda's cart!), tomatoes and peppers.

### CARBS (STARCHY)

Our preferred starchy carbs include oats (we both eat oatmeal almost every single day!), potatoes, sweet potatoes, squashes, grains, and whole grain breads (Nature's Own Sugar-Free Life bread is the bomb.com!).

### HEALTHY FATS

Eat these (in moderation), just keep an eye on portion sizes because they are higher in calories and are easy to overeat without realizing it! Our favorites include avocados, nuts, nut butters, seeds, EVOO, salmon, and cheese.

### FLAVORINGS/SEASONINGS/CONDIMENTS

Use our healthy swaps and the condiments in the recipe section to save hundreds of calories without sacrificing flavor. Aim for spices, herbs or seasonings instead of marinades or high calorie salad dressings.

### DON'T BUY LIQUID CALORIES!

Instead, opt for water, tea, coffee, seltzer, unsweetened nut-based milks or skim milk. (But do treat yo'self to the occasional glass of vino or beer. Because....balance).

**PRO TIP**

We make big batches of protein and freeze a portion of it. It helps us reduce waste and then we can defrost it and use it later for the second half of the week.

# HEALTHY SWAPS & ALTERNATIVES

Remember that small changes have power to make a huge difference when it comes to progress, so we suggest putting in a little effort up front so that you are fully aware of what you are eating. The things that seem little can add up and become big things which set you back from achieving your goals.

Lots of times, there is a lower calorie alternative to what you are eating or habitually using. Over time, we have found lower calorie options to our favorite foods so we can enjoy our food, stick to our goals and maintain our physiques.

Salad dressings, marinades, condiments, sauces and liquid calories are usually the top suspects for hidden calories. On the following pages, we wanted to share our top swaps and how to make meals lower in calories and healthier!

### GROUND TURKEY VS. GROUND BEEF

4 oz (99/1) extra lean ground turkey: 120 calories, 1g fat
4 oz (93/7) lean ground turkey: 170 calories, 8g fat
4 oz (80/20) ground beef: 290 calories, 23g of fat

### AVOCADO VS. MAYO / BUTTER / OIL

1 cup Avocado: 234 calories
1 cup Mayo: 1,495 calories
1 cup Butter: 1,627 calories
1 cup Oil: 1,910 calories

### VEGGIE NOODLES/RICE VS. NOODLES/PASTA/RICE

1 cup of Spaghetti Squash: 31 calories
1 cup of Zucchini: 33 calories
1 cup of Pasta: 130 calories
1 cup of Cauli Rice: 20 calories
1 cup of White Rice: 205 calories
1 cup of Brown Rice: 216 calories

### GREEK YOGURT VS. SOUR CREAM

1 Serving of Greek Yogurt: 60 calories
1 Serving of Sour Cream: 193 calories

**PRO TIP**

Make the sacrifices that are worth it for YOU! If you love white rice, don't force yourself to cut calories and eat cauliflower rice if you think it tastes gross. Find the substitutions that work for you and your preferences and you won't have to choke down things you don't like!

### LETTUCE WRAPS VS. TACO SHELL OR HAMBURGER BUNS

Lettuce Wrap: 5 calories
Taco Shell: 70-180 calories
Hamburger Bun (which is most likely toasted with butter): 200-250 calories

### APPLESAUCE VS. SUGAR

1 cup of unsweetened applesauce: 103 calories, 23g of sugar
1 cup of sugar: 773 calories, 200g of sugar

### PLANT-BASED MILK VS. DAIRY MILK

1 cup of unsweetened almond/cashew milk: 30 calories
1 cup of dairy milk: 100 calories

### PLANT BASED SWEETENER VS. SUGAR

1 cup of plant based sweetener: 0 calories, 0 sugar
1 cup of sugar: 773 calories, 200g of sugar

### CELERY/BABY CARROTS WITH GUACAMOLE VS. CHIPS

1 serving of carrots: 35 calories
1 serving of chips: 110-180 calories

### LOW CAL ICE CREAM OR NICE CREAM VS. REGULAR ICE CREAM

1 pint of low calorie ice cream: 250-340 calories
1 pint of nice cream: 150-300 calories
1 pint of regular ice cream: 1,200-1,520 calories

1 pint of low calorie ice cream: 250-340 calories
1 pint of nice cream: 150-300 calories
1 pint of regular ice cream: 1,200-1,520 calories

### MACRO FRIENDLY SALAD DRESSINGS (2TBSP SERVING)

Trader Joe's Green Goddess Salad Dressing - 20 cal
Olive Garden light Italian dressing - 30 cal
Trader Joe's Almond butter turmeric salad dressing - 60 cal
Kraft Greek vinaigrette - 50 cal
Annie's Organic Lite Honey Mustard - 45 cal

# RECOMMENDED SUPPLEMENTS

You don't need any supplements, but we have a few staples that we use daily to aid in our health, performance, recovery and to fill the gaps in our diet.

Supplements are meant to supplement your diet. They are probably of lowest importance on the health and wellness totem pole. They help to fill the gaps, but we absolutely do not recommend replacing or filling the majority of your diet with them!

If you have the resources and money to spend, here's a few we recommend:

## FISH OIL

Omega 3's are rich in DHA and EPA, two powerful fats responsible for things like increased metabolism, fat loss, and reducing our risk for a host of diseases (cardiovascular disease, cancer, and diabetes).

## VITAMIN D

Vitamin D helps with seasonal depression and can aid in immune and energy levels.

## MULTI-VITAMIN

A multi-vitamin will help to fill gaps in your diet and help restore vitamin or mineral deficiencies.

## PROTEIN POWDER

Not necessary if you get enough protein from whole foods, but if you struggle to hit your protein target (.7-1g per lb of bodyweight), then adding protein powder can be helpful. See how to incorporate protein powder into your diet in previous pages.

## PROBIOTIC

A probiotic will help improve digestion and maintain healthy gut bacteria. Probiotics are especially helpful for those who don't consume dairy or minimal probiotic-rich foods.

## GREENS POWDER

This will help fill the gaps in your fruit or veggie intake. While it can't replace a diet sufficient in fruits or vegetables, greens powder can be extremely helpful, especially if you're on the go. We use them especially when we travel.

## COLLAGEN

It is a highly abundant structural protein in our body that aids in digestion, gut health, glowing skin, healthier hair, stronger nails, keeping bones healthy and strong, and better joint health. We use an unflavored powder and add it to our morning oatmeal...it dissolves completely and is tasteless.

## MAGNESIUM

An essential mineral and the second most abundant electrolyte in the body. The majority of the population is deficient in magnesium. Healthy levels of magnesium can be protective against depression and ADHD, while reducing blood pressure and improving insulin sensitivity.

# MAKING WHOLE FOODS TASTE GOOD

We've heard from so many people that they don't like the taste of vegetables or fruits, or that their food always tastes boring when they try to eat healthy, nutritious meals. We find that hard to believe. After years of experimenting with food and trying to be the best version of ourselves as possible, we've learned that healthy, whole foods can be really delicious, too!

Here's how we've learned to make whole foods (like fruits, veggies, whole grains, and lean proteins) taste so good you'll feel like you're eating something indulgent.

## DON'T SKIMP ON THE SPICES

Most spices have virtually no calories, but are bursting with flavor. Find some spices you love and use them freely on whole foods. Create a variety of stir fry meals with curry or taco seasoning. Add cinnamon and nutmeg to protein shakes and oatmeal. Give any meal a kick with chili powder and red pepper flakes, or add a smoky flavor with paprika and cumin.

## MARINADES AND HOMEMADE DRESSINGS ARE YOUR FRIEND

While you do have to be careful with store-bought marinades and dressings, you can easily make low-calorie versions at home. There are several options in the *Condiments & Spices* section of this book. Once you get comfortable making some of those, experiment with making your own based on the flavors you like! Make sure to keep the oils to a minimum and add a punch of flavor with other low-calorie options like tomato sauce, garlic, ginger, powdered peanut butter, and citrus.

## ROAST 'EM

Roasted veggies add a really great flavor profile beyond just the boring pan-sauteed versions. Sometimes you don't even need any spices beyond salt and pepper! Some of our favorites include roasted broccoli, Brussels sprouts, zucchini, carrots, and sweet potatoes. For even more added flavor, sprinkle with your favorite spices and seasonings.

# OUR ALL-TIME FAVORITE BRANDS & PRODUCTS

There are a few brands and products we've grown to love over the years. At any given time, you can find almost all of these brands and products in our pantry or refrigerator! Many of these are even used to create the recipes in the following pages. The brands in green are linked directly for you so you can shop right away! Many of the others can be found at your grocery store.

**Bob's Red Mill Old-Fashioned Rolled Oats**
**Bob's Red Mill Steel Cut Oats**
**Bowmar Nutrition Blueberry Cheesecake Protein Powder**
**Bowmar Nutrition Hot Chocolate Protein Powder**
Monk Fruit Sugar
Nature's Own Life Sugar-Free Bread
**PEScience Snickerdoodle Protein Powder**
**PEScience Vanilla Protein Powder**
Siggi's Vanilla Yogurt
**Simple Truth Almond Butter**
**Simple Truth Unsweetened Almond Milk**
Swerve Sweetener Replacement
Truvia Brown Sugar Baking Blend
**Vital Proteins Collagen Powder**

# OATMEAL IDEAS

*I love oatmeal. To me, it's not boring.*

**ALAN ALDA**

*Oatmeal is such a great nutrient-packed meal for breakfast, contrary to what many people think. Yes, oats have carbs in them, but paired with some great protein and micronutrient sources, it's a balanced option that is also quick and easy to make. For each of the recipes listed below, just add desired amount of hot water and mix well! For the slow cooker options, just dump all ingredients into a slow cooker and leave it alone for a few hours! The slow cooker options are great to make in bulk, and a perfect way to meal prep your breakfasts on your day off.*

### MEXICAN HOT CHOCOLATE OATMEAL

¼ c. old-fashioned oats
1 serving vanilla yogurt
1 scoop collagen powder
½ serving Bowmar hot chocolate protein powder
2 tsp. ground cinnamon
½ tsp. chili powder
Pinch of cayenne pepper (optional)

---

### SUGAR COOKIE OATMEAL

¼ c. old-fashioned oats
1 serving vanilla yogurt
1 scoop collagen powder
½ serving vanilla protein powder
2 tsp. ground cinnamon
½ tsp. almond extract (or vanilla would work, too!)

---

### SAM'S GO-TO OATMEAL

¼ c. old-fashioned oats
1 scoop collagen powder
1 serving Bowmar blueberry cheesecake protein powder
¾ c. frozen mixed berries
1 tbsp. almond butter
¾ c. riced cauliflower

### COOKIE DOUGH OATMEAL

¼ c. old-fashioned oats
1 serving vanilla yogurt
1 scoop collagen powder
½ serving Pescience Snickerdoodle protein powder
2 tsp. ground cinnamon
2 tbsp. unsweetened dark chocolate chips

---

### CINNAMON RAISIN SLOW COOKER OATMEAL

1 c. steel cut oats
4 c. nut milk
2 c. water
1 tbsp. vanilla extract
2 servings vanilla protein powder
2 tsp. cinnamon
1 tsp. nutmeg
½ c. raisins
½ c. chopped pecans
1 tbsp. molasses

### SUMMER SQUASH SLOW COOKER OATMEAL

1 c. steel cut oats
1 yellow squash, diced
1 serving vanilla protein powder
1 tsp. vanilla extract
2 tsp. Truvia brown sugar baking blend
2 c. nut milk
1 tsp. cinnamon
1 tsp nutmeg

---

### TRAIL MIX SLOW COOKER OATMEAL

1 c. steel cut oats
3 c. nut milk
2 apples
½ c. raisins
2 servings vanilla protein powder
½ c. chopped pecans
1 tbsp. molasses
1 tbsp. ground cinnamon

# PROTEIN SHAKE IDEAS

*The best feeling in the world is a hard workout, a shower, and a protein shake.*

**MIRKO CRO COP**

*As you've probably learned by now, protein is king when it comes to creating a healthy, balanced diet. Shakes are a really easy way to pack in some extra grams of protein each day, just make sure you aren't using them as a major protein source - your major protein sources should be coming from whole foods. These shake ideas each include whole foods to add a micronutrient boost. For each recipe, simply place all ingredients in a blender with desired amount of ice and blend to desired consistency! Feel free to add more nut milk to them if you prefer, too.*

### LIME AVOCADO SHAKE

Juice of 1 lime
1 tsp. lime zest
Handful of fresh spinach
½ an avocado
1 serving vanilla protein powder
1 scoop collagen powder
1 c. nut milk

### PUMPKIN SPICE SHAKE

1 tbsp. nut butter
2 tsp. pumpkin spice (See *Condiments & Spices*)
1 serving vanilla protein powder
1 serving ground flaxseed
1 tsp. almond extract
1 c. nut milk

### BANANA BREAD SHAKE

1 tbsp. nut butter
½ banana
1 serving PEScience Snickerdoodle protein powder
2 tsp. hemp hearts
1 tsp. almond extract
1 c. nut milk

---

### COOKIE DOUGH SHAKE

1 tbsp. nut butter
2 tsp. ground cinnamon
1 serving PEScience Snickerdoodle protein powder
1 tbsp. ground flaxseed
1 scoop collagen powder
1 c. nut milk

### GREEN POWER SHAKE

1 tbsp. chia seeds
1 tsp. cinnamon
1 serving vanilla protein powder
Handful of fresh spinach
¼ apple, cut into chunks
1 scoop collagen powder
1 c. nut milk

### SWEET POTATO SHAKE

1 tbsp. ground flaxseed
1 tsp. cinnamon
1 serving vanilla protein powder
½ c. mashed sweet potato, cooled
1 scoop collage powder
1 c. nut milk

---

### APPLE PIE SHAKE

1 tbsp. nut butter
1 tsp. ground cinnamon
1 tsp. almond extract
1 serving vanilla protein powder
2 tsp. hemp hearts
½ an apple, cut into chunks
1 c. nut milk

### SPICY CHOCOLATE SHAKE

2 tsp. cinnamon
Pinch of cayenne pepper
1 serving chocolate protein powder
1 tbsp. chia seeds
1 scoop collage powder
1 c. nut milk

### AMANDA'S GO-TO SHAKE

2 tsp. cinnamon
Pinch of nutmeg
1 serving vanilla protein powder
Handful of fresh spinach
1 tbsp. nut butter
1 scoop collagen powder
1 c. nut milk

# BREAKFAST

*What nicer thing can you do for somebody than make them breakfast?*

**ANTHONY BOURDAIN**

# BREAKFAST FRIED RICE

*This is a great breakfast option when you're craving something savory!*

1 c. cauliflower rice
½ tbsp. sesame oil
2 eggs
½ c. mixed diced carrots and green peas
¼ yellow onion, dice
1 cajun andouille sausage link, cooked and sliced
1 tbsp. liquid aminos (or low-sodium soy sauce)
Salt and pepper to taste
2 tsp. toasted sesame seeds (optional)

YIELDS 1 SERVING

35G PROTEIN

17G CARBS

31G FAT

465 CALORIES

Heat the sesame oil in a medium pan. Add the diced onion and stir frequently until onions turn translucent and begin to brown.

---

Add carrots, peas, and cauliflower rice to the pan. Sauté until all vegetables are fully heated.

---

Whisk eggs together in a small bowl and season with salt and pepper. Pour eggs into vegetable mixture and stir frequently until eggs are scrambled into the mixture.

---

Add cooked sausage slices and liquid aminos and mix to combine.

---

Sprinkle with toasted sesame seeds.

# CHEESY VEGETABLE EGG MUFFINS

*This is a great option when you have a busy week ahead. Make a batch or two ahead of time and grab them before you head out the door!*

12 eggs
1 c. fresh baby spinach
1 c. low-fat cottage cheese
½ c. low-fat shredded cheddar cheese
1 red bell pepper, diced
2 tsp. paprika
Salt and pepper to taste
Cooking spray
Hot sauce (optional)

YIELDS 6 SERVINGS

21G PROTEIN

5G CARBS

12G FAT

206 CALORIES

Preheat oven to 350 degrees and spray a muffin tin with cooking spray.

---

Place eggs, cottage cheese, paprika, and salt and pepper in a blender and blend until combined.

---

Quickly chop the spinach and fold the spinach, cheddar cheese, and bell pepper into the egg mixture.

---

Divide mixture evenly in the muffin tins.

---

Bake for 30-35 minutes, until eggs are set and begin to brown around the edges.

---

These are great with a little hot sauce on top!

# SPINACH, BACON & CHEDDAR FRITTATA

*Easily turn this frittata into grab-and-go muffins by using a muffin tin instead of a pie dish!*

8 eggs
1 onion, diced
½ c. low-fat shredded cheddar cheese
2 c. fresh baby spinach
½ c. low-fat cottage cheese
8 slices low-sodium bacon
2 tbsp. almond flour

YIELDS 4 SERVINGS

29G PROTEIN

7G CARBS

26G FAT

383 CALORIES

Preheat oven to 350 degrees and spray a pie dish with cooking spray.

In a medium bowl, whisk eggs and season with salt and pepper. Set aside.

Cook bacon to desired crispness in a large pan. Once done, set aside on a paper towel-lined plate to cool. Discard the bacon grease.

Using the same pan, cook your onions until translucent and edges begin to brown.

Add onions, cheddar cheese, spinach, and almond flour to eggs and mix well.

Crumble the bacon and place in a layer on the bottom of the greased pie dish. Pour egg mixture on top.

Bake for 40-45 minutes until eggs have set.

# TURKEY & VEGETABLE SCRAMBLE

*A quick and easy breakfast that is still warm and comforting! Easily double or triple the recipe for meal planning or guests.*

2 eggs
2 egg whites
4 oz. ground turkey
1 bell pepper, diced
½ yellow onion, diced
1 c. fresh baby spinach
½ c. Brussels sprouts, quartered
½ tbsp. olive oil
Salt and pepper to taste

Heat olive oil in a medium pan. Add diced onions and bell peppers and sauté, stirring frequently, until they begin to soften.

---

Add ground sausage to pan and cook, chopping sausage into small pieces as it cooks.

---

Once sausage is cooked all the way through, add quartered Brussels sprouts to pan and season with salt and pepper. Cover and cook until Brussels sprouts begin to soften, stirring occasionally.

---

In a small bowl, whisk eggs and egg whites and season with salt and pepper.

---

Add eggs and spinach to pan and stir frequently until eggs are scrambled and spinach is wilted.

YIELDS 2 SERVINGS

23G PROTEIN

7G CARBS

16G FAT

265 CALORIES

# TEX MEX BREAKFAST BOWLS

*Mexican food is good any meal of the day, am I right or am I right?*

2 eggs, cooked however you'd like (sunnyside up is great on here!)
½ potato, diced small
4 oz. ground turkey
1 tbsp. taco seasoning (See *Condiments & Seasonings*)
½ c. water
1 tomato, diced
1 jalapeno, diced
¼ avocado, sliced
1 c. spinach
½ tbsp. olive oil
¼ c. low-fat shredded Colby Jack cheese
Salt and pepper to taste
Salsa (optional)

YIELDS 2 SERVINGS

23G PROTEIN

13G CARBS

18G FAT

305 CALORIES

Heat olive oil in a medium pan. Add diced potatoes and season with salt and pepper.

---

In a separate pan, cook ground turkey, breaking into small pieces as it cooks. Once turkey is done all the way through, sprinkle with taco seasoning and add water. Stir to combine and let simmer until water has been absorbed.

---

To assemble your bowl, divide spinach between two bowls. Top with ground turkey, potatoes, jalapeno, avocado, cheese, and egg on top. Serve with salsa.

# BANANA MUFFINS

*These are so easy to make and so good! Pair one with half a protein shake for a comforting protein-packed breakfast.*

2 ripe bananas
1 ½ c. almond flour
1 serving vanilla protein powder (we love PEScience!)
½ c. nut milk
½ tbsp. coconut oil, melted
2 tsp. baking powder
1 egg
2 tsp. vanilla extract
½ tbsp. cinnamon
½ tsp. nutmeg
Cooking spray

YIELDS 6 SERVINGS

12G PROTEIN

15G CARBS

16G FAT

243 CALORIES

Preheat oven to 350 degrees. Line a muffin tin with cupcake liners, and/or spray with cooking spray.

---

In a medium bowl, mash bananas with a fork. Add coconut oil, nut milk, egg, and vanilla extract and mix well.

---

In a separate bowl, whisk together the almond flour, protein powder, baking powder, cinnamon, and nutmeg.

---

Pour the liquid mixture into the dry mixture and stir until just combined.

---

Divide the batter between the muffin tins and bake for 18-20 minutes, until a toothpick inserted comes out clean.

# BANANA SPICE PANCAKES

*Did someone say brunch? These pancakes are a guilt-free brunch option that have a little extra oomph of protein added.*

1/3 c. coconut flour
6 eggs
3 ripe bananas
1 serving vanilla protein powder
½ tbsp. cinnamon
1 tsp. nutmeg
1 tsp. ginger
1 tsp. vanilla extract
Cooking spray

In a medium bowl, mash bananas with a fork. Add eggs and vanilla extract.

In a separate bowl, whisk together the coconut flour, protein powder, cinnamon, nutmeg, and ginger.

Pour the liquid mixture into the dry mixture and stir until just combined.

Spray a large pan with cooking spray and heat on the stove. When the pan is warm, pour batter into small discs. When the tops of the pancakes begin to form small bubbles, flip them and let cook another 2-3 minutes.

YIELDS 4 SERVINGS

18G PROTEIN

34G CARBS

10G FAT

307 CALORIES

# TURKEY SWEET POTATO HASH

*A great option for a savory breakfast that is also warm and comforting. Easily prep this one in advance and store in Tupperware for a grab-and-go breakfast option.*

2 sweet potatoes, diced small
1 red bell pepper, diced
1 yellow onion, diced small
2 tsp. paprika
2 tsp. taco seasoning (See *Condiments & Spices*)
¼ c. water
Salt and pepper to taste
8 oz. ground turkey
4 eggs, cooked however you desire (we like over-easy!)
Cooking spray

Preheat oven to 425 degrees. Line a baking sheet with aluminum foil and spray with cooking spray and sprinkle with salt and pepper. Spread the sweet potatoes, bell peppers, and onions on the baking sheet and sprinkle with salt, pepper, and 1 tsp. paprika. Roast the vegetables until sweet potatoes are tender and brown on the edges, about 30-35 minutes.

---

Meanwhile, spray a pan with cooking spray. Add the ground turkey and cook, breaking into small pieces. When the turkey is completely done, add the water and taco seasoning to the pan and continue to cook, stirring to coat. Once the water is absorbed, remove turkey from heat.

---

To assemble the bowls, divide vegetables between 4 bowls, top with the ground turkey, and place an egg on top.

YIELDS 2 SERVINGS

20G PROTEIN

20G CARBS

13G FAT

273 CALORIES

# VEGETABLE POWER BOWL

*This power bowl is loaded with veggies and protein to give you a burst of energy and keep you feeling full through the morning!*

2 eggs
¼ c. nut milk
2 c. fresh baby spinach
½ red bell pepper, diced
¼ yellow onion, diced
½ c. Brussels sprouts, halved
½ tomato, diced
¼ avocado, sliced
Salt and pepper to taste
1 tsp. minced garlic
1 tsp. paprika
½ tbsp. olive oil

YIELDS 1 SERVING

21G PROTEIN

39G CARBS

23G FAT

383 CALORIES

Heat the olive oil over medium heat. Add the diced onion, bell pepper, garlic, paprika, Brussels sprouts and salt and pepper. Cook, stirring frequently, until onions begin to turn translucent and peppers begin to soften.

---

In a small bowl, whisk the eggs, nut milk, and salt and pepper. Pour in the pan with vegetables, and cook, stirring frequently until eggs are done.

---

To assemble, place egg and vegetable mixture in a bowl and top with diced tomatoes and avocado slices.

# OPEN-FACED BREAKFAST SANDWICH

*Sometimes you really just need a sandwich. This breakfast version, with half the bread of a standard sandwich, is packed with all sorts of good-for-you foods and nutrients.*

YIELDS 1 SERVING

12G PROTEIN

17G CARBS

13G FAT

293 CALORIES

1 slice whole wheat bread
1 egg, cooked however you'd like (sunnyside up is our preferred choice!)
1 turkey sausage patty, cooked
1 slice tomato
Small handful of spinach
¼ avocado, sliced
Salt and pepper to taste

Toast the bread.

---

Mash the avocado with a little salt and pepper, and spread on the toasted bread. Top with spinach, tomato, sausage patty, and egg.

# B.A.S.

*I wish my name was Cobb.*
*Then they would send over a Cobb salad.*

**SHIRLEY TEMPLE**

# BRUSSELS SPROUT SALAD

*My love affair with roasted vegetables on salad began a few years ago when I had them on a salad at a restaurant. It basically changed my salad game. This is one of my favorites!*

1 c. Brussels sprouts, halved
½ yellow onion, diced
1 tbsp. olive oil
4 strips low-sodium bacon, cooked
4 hard-boiled eggs
4 c. fresh baby spinach
2 tbsp. ginger dressing (see *Condiments & Seasonings*)
Salt and pepper to taste
Cooking spray

YIELDS 2 SERVINGS

21G PROTEIN

9G CARBS

24G FAT

338 CALORIES

Preheat oven to 415 degrees. Line a baking sheet with aluminum foil and spray with cooking spray. Sprinkle with salt and pepper. Spread halved Brussels sprouts on baking sheet and sprinkle tops with salt and pepper.

---

While Brussels sprouts are roasting, heat olive oil in a small pan. Add onion and cook until they become translucent and begin to brown on the edges.

---

To assemble your salad, divide spinach in two bowl. Top with Brussels sprouts and onions. Crumble bacon on top, cut eggs in half and place halves around the edge. Drizzle ginger dressing on top.

# ROASTED VEGETABLE & SAUSAGE KALE SALAD

*Kale is such a hearty green for salads. It's the perfect pairing for the sweet potatoes and sausage in this salad, creating an explosion of flavors, and cooking the quinoa in bone broth instead of water adds an extra punch of protein.*

4 c. kale
2 tbsp. olive oil, divided
Juice of 1 lemon
1 sweet potato, peeled and diced
8 oz. spicy ground sausage, cooked
1 c. quinoa
2 c. bone broth
Salt and pepper to taste

YIELDS 2 SERVINGS

23G PROTEIN

7G CARBS

16G FAT

265 CALORIES

Preheat oven to 400 degrees. In a bowl toss sweet potatoes with olive oil and season with salt and pepper. Spread sweet potatoes on a baking sheet and bake for 20 minutes, or until they are tender when poked with a fork.

---

Meanwhile, add quinoa and bone broth to a pot. Bring to a boil. Once boiling, reduce to a simmer and cover, cooking until liquid is absorbed.

---

Place chopped kale and lemon juice in a bowl and massage kale to soften it.

---

To assemble the salad, divide kale into two bowls. Top with roasted sweet potatoes, sausage, and quinoa.

# TACO SALAD BAR

*Every night is a good night for tacos! And when it's in salad form, and loaded with veggies, you can have it every night of the week.*

4 c. spring mix
2 tbsp. taco seasoning (see *Condiments & Spices*)
8 oz. protein of choice (chicken, beef, ground turkey), cooked
1 tomato, diced
1 avocado
Juice of two limes, divided
Zest of 1 lime
1 jalapeno, diced
1 tbsp. cilantro, divided
¼ red onion
1 tsp. minced garlic
1 c. black beans
½ c. shredded low-fat Colby-Jack cheese
Salsa

YIELDS 2 SERVINGS

23G PROTEIN

7G CARBS

16G FAT

265 CALORIES

# HAWAIIAN BBQ CHICKEN SALAD

*The flavors in this salad are a little bit sweet and a little bit salty. So basically, you can't go wrong. It's a perfect meal for using up leftover chicken breast, too!*

YIELDS 2 SERVINGS

32G PROTEIN

36G CARBS

19G FAT

438 CALORIES

4 c. spring mix
8 oz. chicken breast
½ red onion, diced
½ c. BBQ sauce (See *Condiments & Spices*)
½ c. fresh pineapple, cut into chunks
1 avocado
1 tbsp. fresh pineapple juice
1 red bell pepper, diced

Bring a pot of water to a boil. Add the chicken breast and boil until chicken is cooked through completely. Set aside to cool.

Once chicken has cooled, use a fork to shred it. Add BBQ sauce and mix well.

In a small bowl, mash avocado with pineapple juice.

To assemble your salads, divide spring mix into two bowls. Top with BBQ chicken, red onion, pineapple, mashed avocado, and bell pepper.

# CHICKEN PAD THAI SALAD

*Pad Thai is one of my all time favorite meals, but I always felt guilty eating it. Now I can have this salad version guilt-free as often as I'd like without compromising any flavor!*

4 c. baby spinach
1 c. bean sprouts
½ c. red onion, diced
1 shallot, diced
8 oz. chicken breast, cubed
½ c. carrots, chopped
½ tbsp. sesame oil
1 tbsp. liquid aminos
4 tbsp. peanut sauce (See *Condiments & Spices*)
¼ c. crushed peanuts
Salt and pepper to taste
Sriracha (optional)

YIELDS 2 SERVINGS

43G PROTEIN

22G CARBS

22G FAT

437 CALORIES

Heat sesame oil in a medium pan. Add shallot and cook until they become translucent. Add chicken and season with salt and pepper. Once chicken is fully cooked, add liquid aminos and stir to coat all pieces.

---

To assemble the salads, divide spinach between two bowls. Add chicken, red onion, and carrots. Drizzle peanut sauce on top and sprinkle with crushed peanuts. Serve with a small dollop of hot sauce.

# AUTUMN SALAD

*This salad combines some of my favorite rich flavors of autumn! It's also loaded with lean protein and healthy fats.*

4 c. baby spinach
2 tbsp. dried cranberries
1 sweet potato, peeled and diced
2 tbsp. walnuts
½ c. red onion, diced
¼ c. blue cheese crumbles
2 hard-boiled eggs
6 oz. chicken breast, cooked and shredded.
Cooking spray
Salt and pepper to taste
2 tbsp. Balsamic Honey Mustard Dipping Sauce
(see *Condiments & Spices*)

YIELDS 2 SERVINGS

34G PROTEIN

32G CARBS

18G FAT

417 CALORIES

Preheat oven to 400 degrees. Spray a baking sheet with cooking spray and sprinkle salt and pepper on top. Spread sweet potatoes on baking sheet and spray additional cooking spray and sprinkle with more salt and pepper. Bake for 20 minutes, or until they are tender when poked with a fork.

---

To assemble the salads, divide spinach between two bowls. Top with sweet potatoes, eggs, walnuts, cranberries, onion, and blue cheese. Drizzle with Balsamic Honey Mustard Dipping Sauce.

# WATERMELON SALAD WITH GLAZED SALMON

*This is such a good summer salad when it's really hot out and you don't want anything too heavy. The watermelon is a refreshing splash of flavor on top!*

9 oz. salmon
1 tsp. minced garlic
2 tsp. honey
4 tbsp. balsamic vinegar
3 tsp. Dijon mustard
4 c. baby spinach
1 1/2 c. watermelon, cubed
1/2 c. feta cheese crumbles
1/2 c. pistachios
1/2 c. cucumbers, peeled and diced
1 shallot, diced
2 tbsp. olive oil
Balsamic Honey Mustard Dipping Sauce (see *Condiments & Spices*)

YIELDS 4 SERVINGS

35G PROTEIN

15G CARBS

31G FAT

469 CALORIES

In a small bowl, whisk together the minced garlic, honey, balsamic vinegar, and Dijon mustard. Place the salmon in a Ziploc bag with the mixture. Refrigerate for at least an hour, and up to 8 hours.

---

Heat olive oil over medium heat in a pan. Add the shallot and cook until translucent.

---

Place the marinated salmon in the pan and cook on each side for 3-4 minutes, or to desired doneness.

---

To assemble your salads, divide spinach between two bowls. Place half the salmon on top, with watermelon, feta, pistachios, and cucumber. Drizzle with Balsamic Honey Mustard Dipping Sauce.

# CUBAN SALAD

*This salad is such a great option for leftover pork! Add even more veggies for an extra boost of micronutrients.*

YIELDS 2 SERVINGS

35G PROTEIN

14G CARBS

12G FAT

272 CALORIES

8 oz. pork, cooked & shredded
4 oz. deli ham
4 c. spring mix or spinach
1⁄4 c. shredded provolone cheese
1⁄2 red onion, diced
1⁄2 c. dill pickle chips
1⁄2 c. tomato, diced
Balsamic Honey Mustard Dipping Sauce (see *Condiments & Spices*)

To assemble the salads, divide the spring mix between two bowls. Top with pork, ham, cheese, diced onion, dill pickles, and tomatoes. Drizzle Balsamic Honey Mustard on top.

# PIZZA SALAD WITH GARLIC CROUTONS

*When you're craving pizza, but don't want to splurge on the real deal, this is the meal for you! Easily add your favorite pizza ingredients to make it your own.*

4 c. spring mix
½ yellow onion, diced
½ tbsp. olive oil
8 oz. ground beef
4 oz. tomato sauce
1 tbsp. dried basil
2 tsp. paprika
Salt and pepper to taste
¼ c. shredded parmesan cheese
½ green bell pepper, diced
2 sliced whole wheat bread, diced
2 tbsp. butter, melted
2 tsp. garlic salt
Tomato Vinaigrette (see *Condiments & Spices*)

Heat olive oil over medium heat. Add diced onion, salt and pepper and cook until onions begin to turn translucent. Add ground beef, dried basil, paprika, and salt and pepper to the onions and cook, breaking into small pieces. Once beef is completely cooked through, add tomato sauce and let simmer while you prepare the croutons.

---

In a small bowl, toss the diced bread with the melted butter and garlic salt. Heat a separate pan and add bread to the pan, stirring frequently until they begin to brown.

---

To assemble salads, divide spring mix between two bowls. Top with ground beef, green peppers, parmesan cheese, croutons, and drizzle with vinaigrette.

YIELDS 2 SERVINGS

33G PROTEIN

25G CARBS

27G FAT

467 CALORIES

# KUNG PAO CHICKEN SALAD

*A savory, spicy salad that is bursting with flavor! If you like spicy food, this will definitely become a weekly favorite.*

8 oz. chicken breast, cut into chunks
1 tbsp. olive oil
1 tsp. crushed red pepper flakes
1 tsp. ginger
1 tsp. cornstarch
1/4 c. bone broth
1 tsp. sriracha
1 tsp. minced garlic
2 tbsp. liquid aminos (or low-sodium soy sauce)
1 tbsp. rice vinegar
1 tsp. sesame oil
1 red bell pepper, diced
1/2 c. crushed peanuts
4 c. spring mix

YIELDS 2 SERVINGS

28G PROTEIN

9G CARBS

13G FAT

271 CALORIES

Heat olive oil over medium heat. Add diced onion, red pepper flakes, and ginger and cook until onions begin to turn translucent.

---

In a bowl, whisk together the cornstarch, bone broth, sriracha, garlic, liquid aminos, rice vinegar, and sesame oil. Add the chicken and stir to coat all the pieces. Pour the mixture into the pan with the onions. Cook until chicken is completely done, stirring occasionally.

---

To assemble the bowls, divide spring mix between two bowls. Top with chicken, red bell pepper, and crushed peanuts.

# MAIN ENTRÉES

*One cannot think well, love well, sleep well, if one has not dined well.*

**VIRGINIA WOOLF**

# PEANUT CHICKEN & VEGETABLE STIR FRY

*An all-time favorite meal of ours. It's easy, adaptable, and the Peanut Sauce makes it so incredibly satisfying.*

8 oz. chicken breast, diced
2 c. fresh broccoli
1 c. carrots, diced
1 red bell pepper, diced
1/2 yellow onion, diced
1 tbsp. sesame oil
2 tsp. minced garlic
1 tbsp. liquid aminos (or low-sodium soy sauce)
1/2 c. Peanut Sauce (See *Condiments & Spices*)
2 tbsp. peanuts, crushed

YIELDS 2 SERVINGS

23G PROTEIN

7G CARBS

16G FAT

265 CALORIES

Heat sesame oil and minced garlic over medium heat in a large pan. Add diced onion and bell pepper, and cook until onion begins to turn translucent.

---

Add chicken to pan and cook, stirring frequently, until chicken is cooked all the way through.

---

Add broccoli, carrots and liquid aminos. Cook until broccoli begins to soften.

---

Drizzle Peanut Sauce on top and stir to coat evenly. Remove from heat.

---

Serve with crushed peanuts on top.

# SWEET & SPICY SOUP

*This soup is loaded with flavor and such a great comforting meal on cold, winter days!*

1 lb. spicy ground sausage
4 c. bone broth
1 sweet potato, peeled and diced
4 c. kale, chopped
Hot sauce (optional, but recommended)

Cook the sausage in a large pot, breaking into crumbly pieces as it cooks.

Once sausage is cooked through completely, add the bone broth and sweet potato. Simmer until sweet potatoes are soft when poked with a fork.

Add chopped kale to the pot and continue to simmer until kale softens, about 5-8 minutes.

Serve with hot sauce. (You don't have to add hot sauce, but you really should).

YIELDS 6 SERVINGS

18G PROTEIN

14G CARBS

22G FAT

363 CALORIES

# SESAME GINGER BEEF & BROCCOLI

*A classic meal that's easy to make, full of flavor, and loaded with protein and green veggies! Mix it up by adding more of your favorite veggies to create a stir fry.*

1 lb. flank steak, sliced
½ yellow onion, diced
2 c. fresh broccoli, chopped
1 tbsp. sesame oil
3 tbsp. minced ginger
2 tbsp. liquid aminos (or low-sodium soy sauce)
¼ c. Ginger Dressing (See *Condiments & Spices*)
Salt and pepper to taste
1 tbsp. toasted sesame seeds

YIELDS 4 SERVINGS

26G PROTEIN

5G CARBS

17G FAT

278 CALORIES

Heat sesame oil over medium heat. Add onions and ginger and cook until onions begin to turn translucent.

---

Add sliced flank steak and cook. Once steak is done, add the broccoli and salt and pepper. Cover and cook until broccoli begins to soften.

---

In a small bowl, mix together the liquid aminos and Ginger Dressing. Pour mixture over the steak and broccoli and stir to coat evenly over low heat.

---

Sprinkle sesame seeds on top. Serve alone or with cauliflower or regular rice!

# ITALIAN GOAT CHEESE STUFFED CHICKEN

*The goat cheese and herbs in this chicken make it so creamy and delicious! This pairs well with a salad or roasted broccoli.*

4 chicken breasts (approximately 4 oz. each)
1 tbsp. olive oil
2 tsp. Italian seasoning
4 oz. soft goat cheese
1 tbsp. fresh basil, chopped
2 tsp. fresh oregano
2 tsp. fresh parsley
¼ c. nut milk
Salt and pepper to taste

YIELDS 4 SERVINGS

32G PROTEIN

1G CARBS

12G FAT

233 CALORIES

In a small bowl, mix together the goat cheese, basil, oregano, parsley, nut milk, and salt and pepper. Set aside.

---

Create a "pocket" in the chicken breasts by using a knife to make a slit on one side. Sprinkle with Italian seasoning.

---

Spoon goat cheese mixture into the pocket of each chicken breast.

---

Heat olive oil over medium heat in a large pan. Add chicken breasts and cook until brown on one side. Flip and cook until browned, and chicken is cooked thoroughly all the way through.

---

Serve with veggies of your choice.

# SPICY SPLIT PEA & SAUSAGE SOUP

*Split pea soup is one of our favorites in the cold winter months, but it definitely lacks protein. This version is the best of both worlds!*

2 c. dry green split peas
3 c. bone broth
1 c. dry white wine
2 tsp. curry powder
1 yellow onion, diced
1 tbsp. olive oil
½ tsp. onion powder
1 tsp. garlic powder
4 Italian turkey sausage links, sliced

Heat olive oil over medium heat in a large pot. Add diced onion and cook until onion begins to turn translucent.

---

Add sausage to the pot and cook until sausage is browned and fully cooked (if you are using uncooked sausage links).

---

Add split peas, bone broth, white wine, curry powder, onion powder, and garlic powder to the pot. Stir to mix well.

---

Simmer until split peas are soft and soup has thickened to desired consistency. If you'd like it to be thicker, turn the heat up for a few minutes. For a thinner consistency, add more bone broth or a little water.

YIELDS 4 SERVINGS

38G PROTEIN

54G CARBS

17G FAT

497 CALORIES

# TEX MEX STUFFED PEPPERS

*A healthy alternative to tacos or burritos, and loaded with veggies. The spices are the perfect blend of Mexican food you are craving, and the peppers add a nice crunch without the chips.*

2 bell peppers
8 oz. ground beef or turkey
½ tbsp. olive oil
2 tbsp. Taco Seasoning (see *Condiments & Spices*)
½ yellow onion, diced
½ c. carrots, diced
1 jalapeno, diced
½ c. Lime Cilantro Diced Tomatoes
¼ c. low-fat shredded cheddar cheese
Juice of 1 lime
½ avocado, sliced
Pinch of sea salt
1 tsp. cilantro (optional)
½ c. salsa

YIELDS 2 SERVINGS

31G PROTEIN

30G CARBS

23G FAT

422 CALORIES

Preheat oven to 350 degrees and line a baking sheet with aluminum foil.

---

Slice the tops off the bell peppers and clean the seeds out. Place peppers in a pot of water and bring to a boil. Let peppers boil for approximately 5 minutes.

---

Remove peppers from pot (use tongs, as the water is probably still very hot!) and place on the lined baking sheet.

*(continued)*

## (TEX MEX STUFFED PEPPERS CONTINUED)

In a separate pan, heat the olive oil over medium heat. Add onion, carrots, and jalapeno and cook until onion begins to turn translucent.

---

Add ground beef or turkey and break into small crumbles as it cooks. Once beef is completely cooked through, add taco seasoning with 1/4 water and the tomato sauce. Stir to mix well.

---

Fill peppers with beef mixture, sprinkle with chese. Bake until cheese begins to brown, about 15 minutes.

---

While peppers are baking, combine avocado, lime juice, salt, and cilantro. Use a fork to break up avocado and combine the mixture. Add salsa and guacamole to peppers just before serving.

# SWEET POTATO SHEPHERD'S PIE

16 oz. ground beef or turkey
4 sweet potatoes, peeled and diced
½ c. bone broth
1 tbsp. cornstarch
1 c. green peas
1 c. shredded carrots
1 yellow onion, diced
1 tbsp. olive oil
¼ c. nut milk
Salt and pepper to taste

Preheat oven to 400 degrees and spray a 9x12 baking dish with cooking spray.

---

In a medium pan, heat the olive oil. Add onions and cook until translucent. Add ground beef or turkey and cook until done completely, breaking into small crumbles as it cooks.

---

In a small bowl, whisk together cornstarch and bone broth. Pour over cooked beef and mix well. Add peas and carrots to mixture.

---

Meanwhile, bring sweet potatoes to a boil in a pot of water. Boil until potatoes are tender.

---

Drain sweet potatoes. Add nut milk and salt and pepper and mash with a fork.

---

Spread beef mixture in the pan and top with mashed sweet potatoes. Bake until potatoes begin to brown, about 25-30 minutes.

YIELDS 4 SERVINGS

28G PROTEIN

38G CARBS

8G FAT

319 CALORIES

# COCONUT CRUSTED CHICKEN TENDERS

16 oz. chicken breast, cut into strips
2 eggs
¾ c. unsweetened coconut
¼ c. panko bread crumbs
Salt and pepper to taste
Balsamic Honey Mustard Dipping Sauce (See *Condiments & Spices*)

Preheat oven to 425 degrees. Line a baking sheet with aluminum foil and spray with cooking spray.

---

Whisk the eggs in a small bowl. Set aside.

---

In a separate bowl, combine coconut, bread crumbs, and salt and pepper.

---

Pat chicken strips dry with a paper towel (this is very important to make sure the coating sticks to them, and so you don't have soggy chicken tenders!).

---

Brush egg wash on both sides of chicken strips, then dredge through bread crumb mixture. Place chicken strips on baking sheet.

---

Bake chicken tenders until completely done, approximately 15-20 minutes.

---

Serve with Balsamic Honey Mustard Dipping Sauce and veggies of choice.

YIELDS 4 SERVINGS

27G PROTEIN

6G CARBS

9G FAT

216 CALORIES

# CHICKEN, SAUSAGE & VEGETABLE PAELLA

*Paella is one of our favorite meals in the world, and this version is easy and healthy. It does take a little time to make, but if it's just a couple of people eating it, you'll have plenty of leftovers!*

YIELDS 6 SERVINGS

26G PROTEIN

27G CARBS

15G FAT

346 CALORIES

2 c. brown rice
3 turkey sausage links
12 oz. chicken breast, cut into chunks
1 c. bone broth
1 red bell pepper, diced
1 yellow bell pepper, diced
1 orange bell pepper, diced
1 yellow onion, diced
2 tbsp. olive oil, divided
½ tbsp. paprika
½ tsp. cumin
½ tsp. saffron
1 c. green peas
1 c. carrots, chopped

Preheat oven to 400 degrees. While the oven is heating, heat 1 tbsp. olive oil in a large oven-safe pan. Add brown rice and stir, cooking rice for 2-3 minutes. Add the bone broth, paprika, cumin, and saffron. Stir to mix well. Reduce heat to low, cover, and let simmer for 20 minutes.

*(continued)*

**(CHICKEN, SAUSAGE & VEGETABLE PAELLA CONTINUED)**

Meanwhile, heat the remaining olive oil in a pan. Add the onion and cook until translucent. Add the chicken and sausage and cook until completely cooked through.

---

Add yellow peppers, orange peppers, red peppers, green peas, and carrots. Stir to mix well and cook until peppers and carrots begin to soften, about 10 minutes.

---

Pour chicken and vegetable mixture on top of the rice mixture. Place the pan in the oven and cook until all the liquid is absorbed, approximately 30-35 minutes.

# CREAMY AVOCADO CHICKEN PARMESAN PASTA

¾ c. whole wheat pasta (or rice pasta), cooked
8 oz. chicken breast, diced
1 tbsp. olive oil
1 tbsp. Italian seasoning
Salt and pepper to taste
1 avocado
Juice of 1 lime
3 tbsp. parmesan
1 yellow onion, diced
½ c. cherry tomatoes, halved
¼ c. pine nuts

YIELDS 2 SERVINGS

36G PROTEIN

44G CARBS

25G FAT

466 CALORIES

Heat olive oil in a pan over medium heat. While oil is heating, sprinkle Italian seasoning and salt and pepper on all sides of chicken breast pieces.

---

Add onion to oil and cook until translucent. Add chicken to pan and cook until chicken is done completely. Add halved tomatoes and stir. Cook for 2-3 minutes, until tomatoes begin to soften. Remove from heat and set aside.

---

Combine avocado, lime juice, and salt and pepper. Add mixture to the cooked pasta and stir to combine well.

---

Add chicken and tomato mixture, parmesan, and pine nuts to pasta. Stir to mix well.

# PUMPKIN CHICKEN CASSEROLE

1 c. whole wheat pasta, cooked
16 oz. chicken breast, diced
1 tbsp. olive oil
2 tbsp. cornstarch
3 c. nut milk
1 tsp. cinnamon
½ tsp. nutmeg
3 ½ c. canned pumpkin
1 c. reduced fat shredded mozzarella cheese

YIELDS 6 SERVINGS

42G PROTEIN

45G CARBS

7G FAT

424 CALORIES

Preheat oven to 350 degrees.

---

Heat olive oil over medium heat. Add chicken and cook until completely done.

---

In a small bowl, whisk together cornstarch and milk and add to pasta with cinnamon, nutmeg, and pumpkin. Mix well.

---

Fold chicken into pasta mixture.

---

Pour chicken and pasta mixture into a 9x12 baking dish. Sprinkle with mozzarella cheese and bake until cheese begins to brown, about 20 minutes.

# EASY WHITE BEAN BURGER

*We love this take on bean burgers! Pair it with your favorite burger toppings and roasted sweet potatoes for a delicious guilt-free meal!*

2 c. navy beans
3 tbsp. olive oil, divided
½ c. panko bread crumbs
1 egg
½ c. yellow onion, diced
1 tsp. minced garlic
2 tsp. chili powder
1 tsp. paprika
1 tsp. cumin
Salt and pepper to taste

Heat 1 tbsp. olive oil in a pan. Add onion, salt and pepper, and cook until they begin to turn translucent. Remove from heat and seat aside.

---

Drain and rinse the navy beans and place in a bowl. Use a fork to mash some of the beans (keep about half of them whole).

---

Once the onions are cooled, add them to the beans along with the bread crumbs, egg, garlic, chili powder, paprika, cumin, and salt and pepper. Use your hands to combine the mixture well.

---

Form the mixture into patties. Using your pan you used for the onions, heat the remaining oil. Place patties in the hot pan and cook a few minutes on one side before turning, flipping only when they begin to brown. Flip carefully and cook until the second side browns.

---

Serve with your favorite condiments and veggies.

YIELDS 6 SERVINGS

6G PROTEIN

15G CARBS

7G FAT

140 CALORIES

# PORK BURRITO BOWLS WITH CILANTRO-LIME BEANS

*This is one of our favorite meals! The crockpot makes cooking the protein super easy. You can even replace the pork with chicken or beef if you prefer!*

2 tbsp. Taco Seasoning (see *Condiments & Spices*)
16 oz. pork shoulder
8 c. leafy greens (spinach & arugula are a great mix with this!)
1 c. low-sodium black beans
Juice of 2 limes, divided
Zest of ½ lime
2 tbsp. cilantro
Salt and pepper to taste
1 tomato, diced
1 avocado
½ red onion, diced
½ c. shredded Colby-Jack cheese
Hot sauce (optional, but so good!)

Place the whole pork shoulder in a crock pot and season with salt and pepper. Cook on low for 6 hours. After 6 hours, use a fork to shred the pork. Sprinkle Taco Seasoning on top and stir to mix well. Continue to cook on low for another 2 hours.

---

Pour the black beans in a sauce pan. Add half the lime juice, lime zest, cilantro, and salt and pepper and stir to mix well.

---

In a small bowl, mix together the avocado, lime, salt, and red onion.

---

To assemble the bowls, divide leafy greens between four bowls. Top with shredded pork, cilantro-lime beans, avocado, tomatoes, cheese, and hot sauce.

YIELDS 4 SERVINGS

36G PROTEIN

20G CARBS

31G FAT

502 CALORIES

# BEANS & FRANKS

*Do these really need any other explanation? I think not.*

1 tbsp. olive oil
1 yellow onion, diced
3 tsp. minced garlic
1 c. unsalted tomato sauce
2 tbsp. molasses
2 tbsp. chili powder
3 tbsp. yellow mustard
1 tbsp. balsamic vinegar
1 ½ cans dark red kidney beans, drained
4 turkey sausage links, sliced

YIELDS 4 SERVINGS

26G PROTEIN

41G CARBS

16G FAT

399 CALORIES

Heat olive oil over medium heat. Add the onion and minced garlic and cook until they turn translucent. Add the turkey sausage and cook until sausage begins to brown on the edges.

---

Meanwhile, in a separate sauce pan mix together the tomato sauce, molasses, chili powder, mustard, and balsamic vinegar over medium heat. Add the kidney beans and stir to mix well.

---

Pour the bean mixture into the pan with the sausage and mix well.

# FLAT OUT ROASTED VEGETABLE PIZZA

*Such an easy, good vegetarian pizza option! You can add more protein if you'd like, too!*

1 Flat Out wrap
¼ c. marinara sauce
¼ c. shredded mozzarella cheese
1 tbsp. fresh basil
½ c. cherry tomatoes, halved
½ c. broccoli florets, sliced
Cooking spray
Salt and pepper to taste

YIELDS 1 SERVING

27G PROTEIN

44G CARBS

14G FAT

236 CALORIES

Preheat oven to 375 degrees. Line a baking sheet with aluminum foil. Spread broccoli on the baking sheet, spray with cooking spray, and sprinkle with salt and pepper. Roast until broccoli begins to brown on the edges, about 20 minutes.

Meanwhile, place the Flat Out wrap directly on the rack of the oven for 2-4 minutes. Remove from the oven. Spread marinara sauce, shredded cheese, basil, and cherry tomatoes on the wrap. When the broccoli is out of the oven, add that to the wrap.

---

Place the "pizza" in the oven on a baking sheet and bake until cheese is melted.

# CITRUS WHITE FISH

*A fresh, citrus flavor that's not too heavy. Pair with a salad for the perfect summertime meal.*

8 oz. white fish filets (such as cod, tilapia, or halibut)
¼ c. fresh orange juice
1 tbsp. orange zest
1 tbsp. liquid aminos
2 tsp. minced ginger
1 tsp. cornstarch
½ tbsp. olive oil
1 lemon, sliced
Salt and pepper to taste

In a small bowl, whisk together orange juice, orange zest, liquid aminos, cornstarch, olive oil, and ginger.

---

Place fish filets in a Ziploc bag and pour marinade over them. Seal the bag and gently rub the marinade onto both sides of the filets. Refrigerate for at least an hour.

---

When you're ready to cook the fish, preheat oven to 450 degrees. Line a baking sheet with aluminum foil and spray with cooking spray. Place filets on baking sheet and add lemon slices on top. Bake until fish is just cooked through, and flaky, about 10 minutes.

---

Serve with a salad or your favorite vegetables.

YIELDS 2 SERVINGS

24G PROTEIN

5G CARBS

6G FAT

176 CALORIES

# GINGER SALMON & VEGETABLE SKILLET

*This is such a flavorful dish! It's so easy and quick to make, which is just an added bonus.*

8 oz. salmon filets
2 tbsp. liquid aminos
Juice of 1 lime
Zest of ½ lime
2 tsp. minced garlic
1 tbsp. minced ginger
1 tsp. honey
½ tsp. garlic chili sauce (or sriracha)
1 tbsp. sesame oil, divided
1 c. sugar snap peas
1 c. carrots, chopped
Salt and pepper to taste

YIELDS 2 SERVINGS

31G PROTEIN

12G CARBS

16G FAT

321 CALORIES

Preheat oven to 425 degrees. While the oven is heating, toss the sugar snap peas and carrots with half the sesame oil, salt, and pepper. Place in a large skillet and put in the oven.

---

Meanwhile, in a sauce pan, whisk together the liquid aminos, lime juice, lime zest, garlic, ginger, honey, and chili sauce and simmer for about 5 minutes until sauce starts to thicken slightly.

---

Brush the filets on both sides with the remaining sesame oil. Remove the skillet from the oven, make a space in the center of the vegetables for the filets, and place filets on the skillet. Drizzle with the ginger sauce. Bake for 8-10 minutes. Let cool before serving.

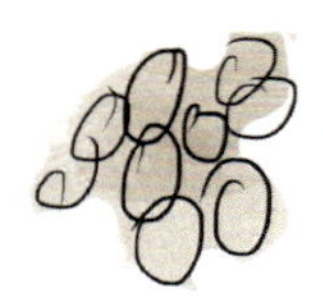

# SNACKS

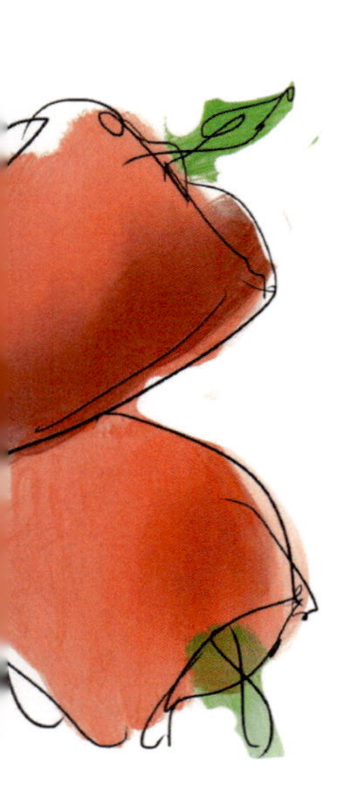

*Even if you're having a snack, enjoying it in a beautiful teacup or on a lovely plate makes it feel like more of an event.*

**MARY HELEN BOWERS**

# CRACK MIX

*You're welcome.*

YIELDS 16 SERVINGS

3G PROTEIN

16G CARBS

10G FAT

154 CALORIES

1 c. whole macadamia nuts
1 c. semi-sweet chocolate chips
1 c. dried blueberries
1 c. yogurt covered raisins

Place all ingredients in a Ziploc bag or tupperware container and shake until mixed.

# CHOCOLATE HAZELNUT ENERGY BARS

*These are so good when you need a quick snack before or after a workout! Keep in an air-tight container for up to a week.*

YIELDS 16 SERVINGS

4G PROTEIN

26G CARBS

15G FAT

235 CALORIES

2 c. pitted dates
2 c. almonds
1 ½ c. unsweetened dark chocolate chips
¼ c. peanut butter
1 tbsp. water
½ c. hazelnuts

Add all ingredients to a food processor and pulse until blended.

---

Lay a piece of parchment paper on a baking sheet. Scrape the mixture out onto the baking sheet. Wet your hands and use them to spread the mixture into a layer that is about 1" thick.

---

Refrigerate for at least two hours before slicing. Slice into bars and store in an airtight container.

# CHICKEN PEPPER POPPERS

*A healthy, macro-friendly take on the familiar jalapeño popper.*

6 mini peppers, halved
½ c. low-fat cream cheese
6 oz. chicken breast, cooked and shredded
½ c. shredded mozzarella cheese
¼ nut milk
1 tsp. garlic powder
Salt and pepper to taste

YIELDS 2 SERVINGS

9G PROTEIN

2G CARBS

4G FAT

75 CALORIES

Preheat oven to 350 degrees and line a baking sheet with aluminum foil.

---

In a small bowl, mix together the cream cheese, shredded chicken, mozzarella, nut milk, garlic powder, and salt and pepper until combined.

---

Place jalapeño halves on baking sheet. Spoon filling into jalapeño halves.

---

Bake until tops begin to brown around the edges, about 15-20 minutes.

# DESSERTS

*I don't share blame. I don't share credit. And I don't share desserts.*

**BEVERLY SILLS**

# CRANBERRY APPLE CRISP

*The tart cranberries in this crisp are a refreshing complement to the sweet apples and crunchy topping. You can also add chopped pecans for a little more crunch!*

1 ½ c. fresh cranberries
½ c. Truvia brown sugar blend
2 apples, diced
1 c. old-fashioned oats
2 tsp. cinnamon
1 tsp. nutmeg
3 tbsp. cold unsalted butter
1 tbsp unsweetened coconut
1 tbsp. coconut flour
Cooking spray

YIELDS 8 SERVINGS

2G PROTEIN

30G CARBS

5G FAT

152 CALORIES

Preheat oven to 350 degrees. Spray an 8x8 dish with cooking spray and set aside.

---

In a saucepan, combine the cranberries, brown sugar blend, and apples. Simmer until the apples and cranberries begin to soften.

---

Meanwhile, in a bowl, combine the oats, cinnamon, nutmeg, coconut, and coconut flour. Add the butter and use your hands to break up the butter and form a crumble.

---

Sprinkle the oat mixture on top of the apples and cranberries. Bake until the topping begins to brown, approximately 30-35 minutes.

# CHOCOLATE CHIP BUTTERSCOTCH COOKIES

2 sticks unsalted butter, softened
1/3 c. Truvia brown sugar baking blend
¼ c. monk fruit sugar
1 package fat-free butterscotch pudding
2 eggs
2 tsp. vanilla extract
1 ¼ c. almond flour
1 ¼ c. coconut flour
1 tsp. baking soda
1 c. unsweetened dark chocolate chips
Pinch of sea salt

YIELDS 12 SERVINGS

5G PROTEIN

25G CARBS

12G FAT

203 CALORIES

Preheat oven to 350. Line a baking sheet with parchment paper.

Cream butter with vanilla, both sugars, and butterscotch pudding in a standing mixer.

Slowly add eggs to the mixer and blend until combined.

In a separate bowl, whisk together both flours, salt, and baking soda. Add this to the wet mixture and mix until just blended.

Fold chocolate chips into the batter with a spatula.

Roll dough in small balls and press flat onto baking sheet. Bake for 10-12 minutes, until edges begin to brown.

# PROTEIN COOKIE DOUGH

*Cookie dough fans rejoice! Not only will you not get salmonella from this version, but it's also healthy!*

¼ c. coconut flour
1 scoop Pescience snickerdoodle protein powder
1 tbsp. Vitacost almond butter
2 tbsp. PB2
½ tsp. salt
½ tsp. vanilla extract
1 tbsp. maple syrup
¼ c. nut milk
¼ c. semi-sweet chocolate chips

YIELDS 4 SERVINGS

9G PROTEIN

18G CARBS

8G FAT

178 CALORIES

In a bowl, whisk together coconut flour, protein powder, PB2, and salt.

---

In a separate bowl, mix almond butter and maple syrup, then microwave for 10 seconds.

---

Stir almond butter mixture over dry ingredients and mix until you get a crumbly texture.

---

Slowly stir in milk until a heavenly dough forms. Fold in chocolate chips.

---

Eat immediately or refrigerate for 2-3 hours for a thicker texture.

# BLUEBERRY NICE CREAM

*There are so many options for creating this nice cream! We're sharing two with you on these pages, but get creative with it and make your own version!*

YIELDS 2 SERVINGS

13G PROTEIN

32G CARBS

1G FAT

178 CALORIES

2 bananas, frozen
1 scoop Blueberry Cheesecake Bowmar protein powder
½ tsp. vanilla extract
¼ c. blueberries (fresh or frozen)

In a blender, blend together banana, protein powder, and vanilla extract. Top with blueberries.

# MINT CHOCOLATE CHIP NICE CREAM

*Another yummy nice cream option for all you mint chocolate chip lovers out there.*

YIELDS 2 SERVINGS

13G PROTEIN

34G CARBS

3G FAT

202 CALORIES

2 bananas, frozen
1 scoop vanilla protein powder
½ tsp. mint extract
1 tbsp. semi-sweet chocolate chips

In a blender, blend together banana, protein powder, and mint extract. Mix in chocolate chips.

# CONDIMENTS & SPICES

*Never go anywhere without condiments.*
*Condiments are our friends.*
**SIMON R. GREEN**

# BALSAMIC HONEY MUSTARD

*Perfect as a sweet and savory dipping sauce or on top of salads as a dressing. Replace the yellow mustard with Dijon mustard for a little extra kick.*

YIELDS 2 SERVINGS

1G PROTEIN

9G CARBS

2G FAT

65 CALORIES

2 tbsp. yellow mustard
2 tbsp. balsamic vinegar
2 tsp. honey
1 tsp. olive oil

Whisk ingredients together in a bowl. Store in the refrigerator for up to a week.

# CLASSIC BBQ SAUCE

YIELDS 8 SERVINGS

2G PROTEIN

14G CARBS

2G FAT

80 CALORIES

½ yellow onion, diced
1 tsp. minced garlic
1 tbsp. olive oil
10 tbsp. tomato paste
½ c. white vinegar
4 tbsp. honey
½ c. yellow mustard
2 tbsp. liquid aminos
1 tbsp. chili powder
1 tsp. cumin

Add all ingredients to a small pot and simmer for approximately 10 minutes, until sauce begins to thicken. Store in the refrigerator for up to a week.

# CREAMY LEMON SAUCE

YIELDS 2 SERVINGS

1G PROTEIN

9G CARBS

7G FAT

102 CALORIES

Juice of 1 lemon
1 tsp. lemon zest
1 tbsp. unsalted butter
1 c. nut milk
2 tbsp. cornstarch

Whisk together cornstarch and nut milk. Set aside.

---

Heat butter in a small pot on low until melted. Add lemon juice, lemon zest, and milk mixture. Continue to simmer for about 10 minutes, whisking frequently. This sauce is best used right away.

# PEANUT SAUCE

*This is an amazing staple sauce for stir fry dishes! It's the perfect blend of sweet and savory, and so satisfying.*

YIELDS 2 SERVINGS

6G PROTEIN

9G CARBS

2G FAT

56 CALORIES

4 tbsp. powdered peanut butter
2 tbsp. water
1 tbsp. liquid aminos
1 tsp. lime juice

Mix powdered peanut butter with water to make a paste. You'll want the consistency to be just slightly thinner than peanut butter.

---

Add liquid aminos and lime juice to peanut butter mixture.

---

Store in the refrigerator for up to a week.

# TACO SEASONING

YIELDS 2 SERVINGS

2G PROTEIN

7G CARBS

1G FAT

43 CALORIES

2 tbsp. chili powder
1 tsp. garlic powder
1 tsp. onion powder
1 tbsp. ground cumin
1 tsp. sea salt
½ tsp. crushed red pepper flakes (optional)

Add all ingredients to a small mason jar, or jar with an airtight lid. Place lid back on jar and shake to mix. Store for up to 6 months.

# PUMPKIN SPICE

YIELDS 2 SERVINGS

1G PROTEIN

11G CARBS

0G FAT

35 CALORIES

3 tbsp. cinnamon
2 tsp. ginger
1 tbsp. nutmeg
1 tsp. allspice
2 tsp. ground cloves

Add all ingredients to a small mason jar, or jar with an airtight lid. Place lid back on jar and shake to mix. Store for up to 6 months.

# GINGER DRESSING

YIELDS 2 SERVINGS

0G PROTEIN

6G CARBS

9G FAT

106 CALORIES

¼ c. avocado oil
3 tbsp. rice vinegar
1 tbsp. liquid aminos
2 tsp. honey
2 tbsp. minced ginger

Whisk together all ingredients in a bowl. Store in the refrigerator for up to a week.

# TOMATO VINAIGRETTE

YIELDS 2 SERVINGS

1G PROTEIN

3G CARBS

7G FAT

77 CALORIES

¼ c. tomato paste
2 tbsp. olive oil
2 tbsp. red wine vinegar
2 tsp. dried basil
1 tsp. dried parsley
Salt and pepper to taste

Whisk together all ingredients in a bowl. Store in the refrigerator for up to a week.

# NOTES

# SOURCES & SPONSORS

If you are looking for more information on a certain topic, we recommend checking out science-based and research driven reliable sources like Examine.com or Precision Nutrition. We don't recommend getting your information from magazines, random Google searches or your friend Karen from HR (sorry, Karen!).

We would also like to thank Vitacost.com for supporting our dream by sponsoring this book. Vitacost.com has been our go-to online shop for years when buying healthy products, and we hope that you use them, too!

**Disclaimer: This book is not intended to diagnose, treat, cure, or prevent any health problem. This is not intended to replace the advice of a physician. Always consult your physician or qualified health professional on any matters regarding your health.**

THANK YOU SO MUCH FOR YOUR SUPPORT AND FOR PURCHASING A COPY OF THIS BOOK!

We know how powerful it is to feel in control of your eating and most importantly, your life. Creating this book has been a milestone for both of us and tangible evidence acknowledging that our stories around food have been rewritten. Publishing this book has been such an emotional experience for both of us and we would love to hear from you if it makes a difference in your life.

Please be sure to get in touch or tag us on social media if you buy the book (and actually enjoy it!).